The Geese Fly High

The Fesler-Lampert Minnesota Heritage Book Series

This series is published with the generous assistance of the John K. and Elsie Lampert Fesler Fund and David R. and Elizabeth P. Fesler. Its mission is to republish significant out-of-print books that contribute to our understanding and appreciation of Minnesota and the Upper Midwest.

Portage into the Past: By Canoe along the Minnesota-Ontario Boundary Waters
by J. Arnold Bolz

The Gift of the Deer by Helen Hoover

The Long-Shadowed Forest by Helen Hoover

A Place in the Woods by Helen Hoover

The Years of the Forest by Helen Hoover

Canoe Country and Snowshoe Country by Florence Page Jaques

The Geese Fly High by Florence Page Jaques

North Star Country by Meridel Le Sueur

Lake Superior by Grace Lee Nute

Listening Point by Sigurd F. Olson

The Lonely Land by Sigurd F. Olson

Of Time and Place by Sigurd F. Olson

Open Horizons by Sigurd F. Olson

Reflections from the North Country by Sigurd F. Olson

Runes of the North by Sigurd F. Olson

The Singing Wilderness by Sigurd F. Olson

The New Way of the Wilderness: The Classic Guide to Survival in the Wild
by Calvin Rutstrum

North American Canoe Country: The Classic Guide to Canoe Technique
by Calvin Rutstrum

Paradise Below Zero: The Classic Guide to Winter Camping
by Calvin Rutstrum

Voyageur Country: The Story of Minnesota's National Park
by Robert Treuer

The Geese Fly High

by
FLORENCE PAGE JAQUES

illustrations by
FRANCIS LEE JAQUES

THE UNIVERSITY OF MINNESOTA PRESS Minneapolis — London

The Geese Fly High was first published in hardcover by the University of Minnesota Press in 1939.

Published by the University of Minnesota Press
111 Third Avenue South, Suite 290
Minneapolis, MN 55401-2520
http://www.upress.umn.edu

A Cataloging-in-Publication record for this book is available from the Library of Congress.

Printed in the United States of America on acid-free paper

The University of Minnesota is an equal-opportunity educator and employer.

12 11 10 09 08 07 06 05 04 03 02 01 00   12 11 10 9 8 7 6 5 4 3 2 1

ACKNOWLEDGMENTS

First of all I wish to acknowledge our gratitude to the National Association of Audubon Societies, which allowed us to visit the Rainey Wild Life Sanctuary, and to Dick Gordon, its superintendent, who exhibited and explained the sanctuary to us and who has been more than generous in his help with the details in the book.

From erudite ornithologists into whose hands this may chance to fall, I plead for tolerance. I claim no expert knowledge of birds, and my observation is delighted rather than profound. But I hope there are no glaring errors. Facts have been checked by my husband and by members of the Audubon staff who are directing the southern sanctuaries — Alexander Sprunt and Robert Allen — and to them I offer sincere thanks.

I am also grateful to Mrs. Anne Stoddard, editor of the *American Girl*, for permission to use the Arkansas material; and to Dr. Robert Cushman Murphy, who has given me permission to quote from his *Oceanic Birds of South America*. The quotation on page 78 from Proust's *Remembrance of Things Past* is reprinted by courtesy of Random House.

FLORENCE PAGE JAQUES

LIST OF ILLUSTRATIONS

The Geese Fly High

Two mallards tumbled out of the windy sky. Lee had made a double. Putting down his gun he began to paddle forward after his birds.

"That's my day's limit. Want to change your mind and try?"

We were in a duck boat on a rice lake in northern Minnesota. After a long canoe trip through the border lakes Lee had found a chance for several days' shooting before we went east, and early that morning we had driven down a rough road through spruce forest and peat bog. The latter seemed to me oddly implacable, for in one place where it had caught fire it had been smoldering for over a year, in spite of winter snows or spring rains.

At the end of a grass-grown road we had made our way through the muskeg to the lake. I had never picked my way across floating bog before, and in the cold morning wind I followed dutifully, for once, in my husband's footsteps. Through the reddish green of the thick muskeg we went, while tangles of bushes caught at us and water traps and muddy pockets made precarious walking. After we passed the last small spruces we leaped, with our guns, like two Elizas with elongated babies, from one yielding clump of muskeg to another, until our vague path vanished in deep mud.

I found then that it was necessary to walk two slippery aspen poles to attain the duck boat.

"What if I slip?"

"It's over your knees at this end, up to your neck at the other," Lee said judicially.

We both made the embarkation successfully, but departure was another matter, for the lake bottom was the same unstable peat as the shore; there was nothing for our paddles to push against. But by one slow inch after another we managed to escape the sticky grasp.

This corner of the lake was full of the wild rice which the ducks like to feed upon, and as we paddled through it the sprangled heads emptied their grains into our boat until we had a small harvest. Beyond the bend we saw a flock of ducks circle and light down. We made our way warily toward them.

Lee had great good luck that day; it was only midmorning when he made his final double and invited me to try my skill. I crawled cautiously over him to the bow seat and sat there tense, determined to fire this time. The day before we had had a gold and tawny afternoon in the stubble fields along the Mississippi, hunting prairie chickens. It had been a glorious time, except when the chickens flew up. Then, no matter how ready my gun was, I was invariably so overcome by the size and whirr of the birds that I remained gaping till they had completely vanished, except for Lee's victims. "It's the dog and not the hunter who's supposed to freeze," Lee had explained patiently. But I couldn't learn.

This time I meant to redeem myself. So I sat alert, exhilarated by the wild and windy day, half sun, half menacing storm. Tall bulrushes and the slender wild rice bowed before an icy northwest wind. My fingers and feet were cold. I shivered with excitement and resolve. I intended to shoot a duck!

Stray lines of them were far off against the gray horizon. Someone was shooting in another lake and putting them up, Lee said. One flock came

4

straight toward us over a jagged line of tamarack and spruce, but it was high and veered before it reached us.

"Look to the left," Lee whispered. A brown bird was slanting fast high over the alders. It dropped swiftly into a close growth of rice.

"See her?" said Lee. "That's a smart mallard. Remember the first ducks — how they circled and fussed around before they lit in? But this one wasn't wasting any time before she found cover. I'll paddle now; a single duck usually hides away when she comes in like that. Let's see if we can find her."

We couldn't. She was hidden in the wild rice, and there she meant to stay. We heard a clamor ahead of us.

"Those fool coots again," Lee muttered.

"I don't see why people scorn coots," I protested.

A regiment of the black waterfowl was massed in the lake ahead. As we paddled forward they rose with one accord and began to run along the surface of the water, taking long strides with their big feet, their chalky bills bobbing and making them look like astonished clowns.

"You shouldn't laugh out loud when you're hunting," Lee told me severely.

We pushed on with difficulty through densities of wild rice. The stalks tangled about us; the sun came out again and gilded the rice heads. Then we reached bulrushes, where smooth stems let us slide easily along until our boat found open water in a little cove.

"Shoot!" Lee called. Two birds flew up before me. I raised my gun. Shoot a little in front of them, I remembered.

"I got it!" I cried triumphantly. This was why people went hunting, this sudden feeling of great achievement, this sense of victory. "I hit it! I really hit it, Lee!"

Lee was laughing. "You shot the coot," he said. "Why pass up the teal?"

"Oh, is it a coot?" I was slightly crestfallen but still proud of myself.

"Couldn't you tell?"

"Heavens, no. I didn't have time to stop and consider what species my ducks were!" I looked at the draggled bunch of feathers and wished it was still running crazily along the water.

"You don't need time. You just know," said Lee, picking up the despised coot reproachfully.

"Not me. You've had a lifelong training in ducks, Lee; you forget how seldom I've seen them. I can't be an expert that way."

"But a coot and a teal! A coot isn't even a duck; it's related to the rails."

"I don't mind," I said comfortably. "I know you couldn't tell an elderberry flower from a blackberry blossom, if they were side by side. It depends on what you've always concentrated on. Why, I've never even seen wild ducks near at hand before, except the mergansers we watched last month."

"That's so," Lee reflected. "You've never had much of a chance at waterfowl."

"My education was only fragmentary," I apologized.

He went on without noticing my levity, "The ducks go south over this part of Minnesota at night — clear cold nights in November." He had found that out quite by accident, he said. When he was a boy he happened to be out at dusk once, hunting for deer. Sitting among the poplars near a clover field he heard a faint clear note, like a wind rising. He looked at the trees, but no breath of air stirred their branches. Looking higher he could still find nothing. Then he saw far overhead a waving line of ducks going south, stretching across the whole sky from east to west. They were so high the individual birds were scarcely visible, even as dots; so high that he would not have heard the sound if the night had not been so still and he had not been listening so intently for a deer. He traced the line across the sky till it was lost, at either end, in the distance. He estimated ten thousand birds — scaups probably. In other years he listened, on still November nights, and heard the same clear sound of passage, but never again did he see such a spectacular migration.

"It's been a long time since I've really studied ducks," Lee said reflec-

8

tively. "And I never have seen enough geese to satisfy me. We might take a long holiday some winter and go down this Mississippi valley, all the way to the gulf."

"I'd like that. Only I don't want to spend the whole holiday being *educated* in ducks," I added, eying him.

"If we go you can find things out for yourself," Lee promised. This was extremely generous, for there is nothing that the bird-minded enjoy so much as telling you that the thing you see or don't see is a boat-tailed grackle or a bristle-thighed curlew. "I've never seen the snow and blue geese, though they come up through Minnesota in the spring; I'd like to track them to their wintering grounds on the Louisiana coast. And you would certainly see waterfowl there!"

So that was why we happened to be driving over frosty Illinois roads in late December, the back of our car piled high with a most heterogeneous load. Two large suitcases, one filled with gala attire, the other crammed with corduroys, sweaters, and rough wools. Two smaller bags, one with overnight needs, the other heavy with field glasses, cameras, and flashlights. One huge canvas parcel was a tent, another was what we hoped would be a boat when it was put together. We also had a medley of fragile Christmas presents, hip boots, a small gasoline stove, a sketching outfit, an evening wrap too bulky for the suitcase, a gun, and a hatbox!

We planned to take two months and make a great circle, west a thousand miles from New York to Illinois for Christmas with my family, then south to the White River bottoms in Arkansas to see the thousands of mallards there. South still farther to the Rainey Wild Life Sanctuary in the heart of the Louisiana marshes to see ducks and geese, east to the Atlantic

9

coast, and from there north to New York again. An immense ring of almost four thousand miles. But the jewel in this ring, our lodestar, was the Louisiana sanctuary, where we would have long days entirely surrounded by marshes and could come to know the wild wings over them.

We were nearing Decatur, and my heart was beginning to beat fast at familiar corners as we sped along between flat snowy fields, a clear afterglow around us. Then we had our first glimpse of wildfowl that winter, long before we expected it — in mid-Illinois, on Christmas Eve!

"Ducks!" Lee said triumphantly.

"They can't be! Where?" I saw a faint black line in the rosy air. Faint, but unmistakable.

"They *are* ducks. I thought you said — "

"We never did see ducks."

"You were never conscious of birds before you knew me — "

"But I would have seen ducks if they'd been here; I saw bluejays and woodpeckers in spite of myself. Why, Lake Decatur must have brought them — it's been made since I left. There was only the Sangamon River when I lived here."

Over a small hill the dark water of the lake showed between snowy banks. We pulled up at the side of a shore road. Slim trees were a frosty white around us, behind them the sky was faintest rose and amber. When Lee lowered the window crystals of icy air rushed in. He scanned the dark gray water with his field glasses.

"There they are — black ducks. In the water and on the ice. Right in the mathematical center of the lake. The black duck is the cleverest duck of all, I tell you. He never misses."

"Let me see." I peered through the glasses at the black dots bobbing on the water. How small they were! How independent and removed from our world! Lee looked again.

"See, there are more lighting in!"

Silhouetted for a moment against the chill air sharp wings slanted to the

water, down the left bank. A beautiful joyous motion it was, as the birds came swiftly down. They gave a touch of wildness to my familiar Illinois, which I had never felt before. Yet in my mood of high expectancy they seemed the symbol of homecoming, too. Always afterwards, whenever I saw ducks first lighting in, a wave of rapturous anticipation swept through me for an instant; I had to stop and think what was making me feel so eager, to realize it was a memory, and not impending joy, that stirred.

"Mallards," Lee said. "They aren't taking much of a chance lighting there. But they aren't as super-cautious as black ducks — "

Decatur was very near. Down a street completely roofed with snow-laden boughs an old house with wide porches was waiting for us. The windows would be yellow-lighted now, with holly wreaths black against them. I liked this first cold glimpse of the wildfowl we were going across the land to seek. I liked the taste of the icy air, the touch of strange loneliness in the twilight. But a touch was enough, on this particular eve.

"Don't you think — " I began tentatively.

"Listen. You can hear them."

Through the still air came a muffled quacking, gentle and conversational. It was engaging, this quaint Christmas carol, as the night came down around us — like the murmur of sleepy children. Children! There were some hilariously awaiting us this minute.

" — and black ducks were even wise enough to become seagoing when they were shot in the marshes — "

"When we came home after we were first married, Lee, Billy was only two. He was jealous, do you remember? He hid upstairs and heaved a half-brick down at you as you came in the door. He's too old to do that now."

"You sound extremely regretful," my husband said. Taking a last look at the black flock on the ice, he started the car toward home.

It really seems self-evident that New Year's Eve, of all festivals, should not be spent in a lonely cypress swamp. But as we were expected at Rainey sanctuary by the first week end in January it was almost a necessity. And the idea of camping out in midwinter, beginning a new year in a tent, had a certain charm. It was unusual, to say the least. It might be fun.

It wasn't.

On the twenty-ninth of December, having left our gay Christmas house party far behind us, we found ourselves in Little Rock, Arkansas. I hadn't liked Arkansas, coming through it. Midwinter is not the ideal time to see midwestern states, of course. But Illinois had been very satisfactory, dazzling us with snowy fields and frosted woods under clear green skies. At its border however we had lost all trace of snow, and a drizzling chilly rain hardly improves any country.

The flat Arkansas roads seemed endless, straight and uninteresting, with a slippery boulevard of mud on each side and a deep ditch beyond that. Along these roads in the deep mud the decrepit cars of negro tenants were wrecked, or broken down, or simply resting, every mile or two. As a rule

they had not gone completely into the water, but balanced on the edge of the ditch in an undecided way that made me acutely uncomfortable.

Little Rock was a pleasant town, I admit. But when the game commissioner there found that my husband wanted to see ducks (and shoot a few perhaps, but the main point of our expedition was to see them) he sent us straight away from Little Rock. We were to go to Stuttgart, then to an even smaller town to find a game warden, who would advise us about getting into the White River bottoms.

The warden looked at us in a puzzled way; women and ducks weren't mixed, in his experience. There was a small settlement of houseboats down the river, he said, but too rough company for a lady; he guessed they'd take us out from there to a camp site, though hunters always stayed on the houseboats or in cabins on high ground. But it was late afternoon — we'd have to wait till tomorrow to start. "And I hope you won't mind the hoot owls, lady; if you haven't heard 'em they'll make your hair stand straight up."

This minute town wasn't so bad. In fact it had a rather endearing ugliness, with hitching posts along each side of a square and old-fashioned general stores. But the hotel was the worst one I had ever encountered. Our room was like one of the ghastly bedrooms in the one-reel comedies of the silent films, except that instead of a bare gas jet we had a kerosene lamp. The bed slats even fell off, one after another, like leaves from a tree.

After a greasy supper we left the hotel gladly when the warden and his wife came to take us for a ride, so that we could hear the ducks through the rice fields. These gluttons, although they eat acorns in the swamps all day, fly in at night to the rice fields to feed there and sometimes make havoc of the crop. It was strange to hear the great quacking clamor invading the quiet darkness of the farm country. Flaring torches went marching through the distant night as men along the fields frightened the feathered pirates away.

The next morning I left our gritty hotel room with a great sigh of relief; surely nothing could be worse than that had been. (How wrong I was!) It was almost a spring morning, with a warm wind, fresh and damp, and above the little town we saw our first flight of wildfowl, a flock of great Canada geese from the Arkansas River country. That long line high in the blue air quickened my pulse.

Out in the backwoods beyond the rice fields our road soon became a mass of deep zigzag ruts, which twisted the car cruelly. The cabins on the main road had been pitiful, but they were gems of purest ray compared with the stricken huts here. A half-wild, half-starved pig, a razorback, running across the road ahead of us, seemed a symbol of the whole country.

At last down around a hill we came to an expanse of muddy shore and a sullen gray-green river. Black trees stood stark along it. There were houseboats along the bank, and a few scattered cabins. I felt drawn to the houseboats, the only cheerful note in this sallow place. Cheerful, indeed: one was done in red, green, and white, with blue trimmings; another's vivid yellow was edged with startling purple. Rather battered as they were when you looked closely, they had a jocund air that was reassuring.

While Lee went to inquire about the region's possibilities I was left in the car. I watched the group of men on the river bank leisurely discussing our fate, and to my surprise I began to feel a little reluctant about this expedition.

Lee came back satisfied. "They're taking us out fifteen miles."

"Out where?"

"Why, out into this flooded swamp. Fortunately they know a point of land that's usually dry."

I got out of the car slowly. This river was not appealing. And fifteen miles into a swamp was too far!

We climbed into a leaky open launch, a flatboat with our luggage trailing behind, and a young guide started off with us. I looked back at the group of men who had decided where we were to camp and felt vaguely resentful. This feeling amazed me; I had always welcomed any chance to camp out before. But the heavy opaque flood with drowned trees rising from it — it really was not a very lighthearted place. Somehow I had expected the

16

White River bottoms to be open grassy country with a river curving widely through it.

We went on through the submerged land, keeping to the course of a muddy branch of the White River. On either side, deep in its flow, were willows and pin oaks and buckbush. When we came to cypress trees with their wide folds of trunk spreading toward the water, ducks began to fly up here and there as we went by. Then the faint sun disappeared in a cloudy bank, and the world became still more somber. This swamp was uninhabited. We passed one small cabin, and that a deserted one, as we wound through river and lagoons and cut through underbrush. We could never find our way back again if the guide mislaid us.

Lee pointed out how blue the mallards looked as they flew away through the cypresses, and discovered a pileated woodpecker, which, he said joyfully, was seen in extremely wild places. He showed me three eagles, strikingly black and white in the pervading gray, flapping off above the tree tops. My heart began to rise out of its despondency and give a few cheerful flaps of its own. After all, this *was* a different place to see.

Great bunches of mistletoe hanging in the branches over us made me remember Christmas was only a few days behind.

> *"God rest you merry, gentlemen,*
> *Let nothing you dismay . . ."*

Certainly not. And we couldn't stay in this swamp, of course; we'd find a different section soon.

For two hours we chugged along. Razorbacks, rooting among the oaks on a soggy bank, were really wild hogs here, the guide said. The sharp-backed creatures seemed to eye us with a furtive malice as we passed. At last, around a bend, a higher point of land emerged. This was our goal, this the scene of our New Year revelry. And we hadn't come to a different country; it was still swamp.

We turned down a bayou of black water, overhung by naked boughs. To the west a narrow channel of water opened through the tree trunks; there was another to the northeast. On the point an open space among the trees seemed large enough for our tent, and the guide edged the launch cautiously among the black stumps to the shore. Soon all our belongings sat diffidently on the bank.

Certainly it was a desolate place, this inert backwater, with pallid trunks rising from it, cast-iron branches barring the sky, damp woods stretching off into a dim blur. The sun had completely vanished. A sudden uproar startled me. What was the barking din? A pack of hounds? "Mallards," the guide said. "They sure squawk here."

The two men pounded our tent pegs down through dead brown leaves, while I made sandwiches. The guide was entranced by our tent and our small gasoline stove; our collapsible boat he hung over ecstatically. I repressed a sudden impulse to shower him with the entire outfit.

Do you know the feeling that comes when, after looking forward to meeting someone, you do meet him, and through the conversation have a vague unease until suddenly you realize it's no good — you aren't liking each other and you never will? I had that feeling now about this place.

Lee began to set up our kayak for the first time, fitting the wooden frame together, stretching the canvas over it, while the guide marveled openly. I sat down in the doorway of the tent. Nearby a green briar trailed through the dead leaves and fallen sticks. It had a pale green stem with tiny thorns, and mottled darker leaves, fresh and crisp. It was something to like in this odd world. I looked at its slight exquisite outline steadily.

It came time for the guide to leave. The motorboat, our last link with the world, started off; the chugs grew fainter and fainter. I found that Lee was looking at me in a worried way. I knew that I had never acted like this before, in any kind of place, and I managed to give a smile of joyful satisfaction, at which he looked more worried than ever. I really made an effort to behave. But the air was so oppressive, warm and heavy and ominous; I wanted to brush it away, like cobwebs. No ripples broke the uncanny stillness of the black water around us. The barking bothered me too. I couldn't remember it was the mallards. I kept thinking, "Hounds after a fox. How can they run through water?"

"Let's go up that branch of the river," said Lee.

Our kayak was not as easy to handle, we found, as our canoe had been, but it amused us immensely. We were buttoned into it so that we were all of a piece, and only a thin layer of canvas separated us from the water; we could feel the waves move under us. I wondered, if we should tip over, whether we could complete the circle and come up smiling, as the Eskimos do.

We paddled along a narrow bayou, past low banks deep in oak leaves, around the flares of cypress boles. Ducks flew up from the water ahead. I began to be excited. Small flocks swept above the bare branches, again and again. Their necks were straight and rigid as iron rods, their wings gave an almost invisible flash. This was a new way to see ducks flying. On the few former occasions when I'd seen their flights, along the Atlantic sea coasts, at Barnegat or Montauk Point, or over the rice lakes in Minnesota, they had been in open air. It seemed strange to me now to see wild ducks darting above tree tops, strange and yet harmonious. Sometimes they were so near that even I could tell they were mallards as they flew over, their emerald heads gleaming, their ruddy breasts and white neck-rings unmistakable. I could hear the sharp whistling of their wings. The lure of ducks — I began to understand it.

At last we came from these backwaters to the White River itself, a cruel and relentless tide in the dim winter afternoon. Here as we peered through the willows we saw first an enormous great blue heron rise up from the water, then a minute Carolina chickadee fly along the twigs; a greater contrast could hardly be imagined. Lingering awhile at the edge of the swamp we looked out on the wide gray current, far too powerful for our frail craft to confront, and then we turned toward our home.

The return was a lovely voyage. The sky had cleared, the late afternoon merged imperceptibly into a sunset of pale gold clouds banding the blue air. In its vast serenity drifted long curves of dotted wildfowl, flung like broken necklaces across the far sky. It was extremely beautiful and still.

Down by our kayak a sudden wind shook the oak trees strongly, and then died down again. Two wood ducks, the most brilliant in plumage of all our wildfowl, flew over us to light among the timber. I marveled at their iridescent green, the white lines setting off feathers of blue and bronze and russet. We heard our first owl, far off, eerie and splendid in its falling cadence.

Later and later. A dim rosy glow shimmered the water now, and myriads of mallards came swiftly over, cutting across the violet clouds. The sound of their wings mingled with the murmur in the trees. They flew endlessly, flock after flock of quarter notes, variations on a single theme, each phrasing lovelier than the last. We kept quite motionless, anchored against a fallen log, and watched the flighting of thousands of these wild birds, till it was night.

It was ghostly then, finding our way back to our tent. A faint star

wavered and then was lost in clouds, and the peace which the afterglow had brought me vanished with it. Darkness and disquietude crept through the underbrush together.

No, this place and I did not understand each other. With our canoe country I had touched hands at once, and I had thought that I could care for any place unmarred by man — desert, brush tangle, stony mountain side. This place I shrank from.

But Hudson himself said of the New Forest, "Yet these woods have a less enduring hold than the open heath. It is a passion, an old ineradicable instinct in us; the strongest impulse in children, savage or civilized, is to go out into some open place." If he could feel imprisoned by the lovely broken glades of that English forest, how could I blame myself for a dislike of this dank swamp where one could not escape a moment from the bars of stripped branches, where one couldn't even run!

In the tent, lit by two feeble candles, Lee put the gasoline stove together while the owls, louder now and more bullying, called outside. We had sardines and kidney beans, buttered bread and oranges, a most unimaginative supper. But my imagination was busy along other lines; I couldn't seem to feel a professional concern. I wanted only to huddle into my sleeping bag with our conspicuous candles out.

All day long I had felt unseen eyes, as you do in some houses — which impel you to whirl and then there is never anyone there. And when our candles were lit it was as if we were in a show window, with the whole bottomland an audience of peering faces. We blew our small lights out at eight o'clock. I went to sleep at once, before I had time to begin to think, and slept straight through till early morning.

Very early morning, for wintertime. Lee woke me at five-thirty. Breakfast seemed delicious, since our supper had been so frugal, and through the raised tent flap while we ate we watched the dark gray night outside grow comfortably lighter and lighter. Already we could hear the ducks talking loudly as they breakfasted on acorns all around our bank. It seemed quite

festive to hear so many breakfast parties. My feeling of desolation had vanished overnight.

After breakfast we waited for the guide who was to take Lee in the launch to shoot. We paced our small terrace, and I felt debonair enough to ask Lee if he thought those wild pigs might be near neighbors? He didn't, so I wandered down the bayou, to find more of my green briar embroidering the steep river bank and to pick up acorn cups like the ones I used to treasure from the autumn woods at home.

At last we heard the launch coming, and our guide hailed us jovially. As we set off, small bands of ducks flew up constantly — I couldn't see why we didn't stop almost anywhere to shoot and concluded it was for a masculine reason impossible for me to understand — and at last we came out into a pale lake where immense cypresses stood knee-deep. Ducks floated at the other end, watching us far too guardedly, while woodpeckers drummed on dead branches and a great eagle soared haughtily above the trees. We twisted back into the swamp again.

Here the guide disappeared mysteriously, leaving us on a narrow bank. We took pictures of cypress boles and reflected trees until he reappeared with a report that there were mallards in a lagoon near by; it would take crawling to get to them; perhaps the lady better stay on the bank. The lady was too proud to protest. She watched them shove off, only saying carelessly, "Don't stay too long, will you?" For if they forgot which bank to find again there was very little to eat in this wilderness and no way to walk home.

Sitting there I watched swarms of tiny silver bubbles drift past the flanges of the cypress trunks; I looked up at the pattern of withered tree tops. How beautiful this place must be in April, when the cypresses are feathery with new branches of the palest green! It would be a fragile study in blue and green and gilt, filled with bird notes. I sat there for a long time, trying to hurl myself forward into spring. But when at last I heard the motor again I became absorbed in my notebook. "No motion anywhere,"

I wrote, completely oblivious of the loud approach. "Water dark gray and lavender; distant brush plum color. The cypress has turquoise and violet shadows in its gray-brown bark." Then the boat swung in to let me aboard and Lee held up three ducks triumphantly.

Back at our tent at noon the guide had lunch with us before he left. How I longed to leave with him! But we had said we'd stay three days; we couldn't face the shanty boats before that time was up. I watched the motorboat disappear for another twenty-four hours.

If I had only said to Lee at first, "This place appalls me," we could have laughed at it together. Instead I had tried to be a stoic, which is a mistake for me; now I couldn't admit my discomfort. Yet Lee knew I was hating the place — I couldn't talk, always a portentous symptom.

The sky cleared. It was a warm and sunny hour, and Lee began to sketch a mallard wing. I covered myself up and went to sleep on the river bank. When I awoke I was no longer haunted by the vision of an old house gay with New Year's bells, crammed with chatter and laughter and bright fires. The afternoon had clouded over again and we went out hunting by ourselves, up along the bayou.

When we came to a lagoon thick with willows we drifted quietly about, in a light rain, trying to surprise the mallards, who swam in pairs through the trailing branches. Many mallards mate before the spring migration, and these seemed to have the happiest companionship. Two by two they voyaged contentedly around the willow stems and between the arches of buckbush. From our boat, so low in the water, they looked majestic, especially the drakes with their green heads and bronze breasts shimmering and the permanent curls in their tails very exact. We didn't want to disturb this little paradise of feathered Eves and Adams. We left it unmolested.

Farther along we came close to a flock of mallards yapping in the timber. Lee tried to crawl up to their small pond from the bank but he had no luck, and we started back.

It was a gray sundown, on this New Year's Eve. In our kayak beneath

the low branches of an oak we watched the ducks pour by in their great squadrons high above us. Their beautiful clear-cut silhouettes speeding past, beyond the subtle pattern of slim twigs, seemed even more startling than the night before. Numberless silver pinions cutting the silver-gray air. Wood ducks flew just across our bow, up the lagoon, their colors bright even at twilight.

The wings of the mallards made a low cooing sound as they flew over. When we moved at last, whole fleets of them in the lagoon dashed through the water before they finally rose up and away. We had silver splatters ahead of us, like fireworks, wherever we turned. At last it was black night, and we groped again along the murky shore to our pale green tent glinting through the trees.

It rained that New Year's Eve. Our stove refused to behave and the campfire we built was a reluctant one. We went to bed after a cold and clammy supper. All night it rained, harder and harder on the tent roof, slackening, promising deceitfully to stop, then rattling down again. The mallards were loud in the woods. I lay awake, hearing sticks crack and leaves crunch in the darkness without, remembering orchestras and rosy lights and confetti.

Then I heard a motorboat.

That may not sound appalling, but it froze my blood. We hadn't heard any boats at all, except once, far off, on the White River itself. What would a motorboat be doing here at night? There wasn't anything to come for. Except us.

I lay tense. The chugging grew faintly stronger. I thought of drunken parties from the shanty boats, out for a practical joke. I thought of those sullen negroes we had seen. An owl hooted ominously, and reminded me I'd heard of river pirates. Then before my wakeful eyes flashed a vision of the Little Rock paper of two days before; it had told of a peculiarly revolting murder, with details only Poe could revel in.   If the murderer had taken refuge in this swamp!   As of course he had: what better place?

The noise of the motor stopped abruptly. That meant without a doubt that they were landing. They were now creeping up on us. Well, Lee could manage one or two — if he'd only untangle himself from his sleeping bag! — but what if there were half a dozen?

A stick snapped and I jumped. Nothing happened. Why didn't they attack? Of course, it might be a maniac prowling around and around us. These gruesome places make people go mad. As Lee would find, I thought with some satisfaction, when he woke to greet me in the morning. "Who? Whoo?" went an owl. "Only a maniac," I answered resentfully.

I knew perfectly well my terror was childish, but "Lee," I whispered, "there was a motorboat. It stopped."

"What of it?"

My terror changed to indignation. I had my own opinion of a husband who would drag a reasonably gentle wife out here. Willfully and premeditatedly. Why had I come to such a ghastly place with this kind of man, who added injury to insult by going placidly to sleep and leaving me to lie in wait for enemies all alone? I almost lulled myself to sleep with exasperation at such unfairness. But then I heard the motorboat start again, and I stiffened with renewed apprehension. Oh, what a New Year's Eve! If only we were sleeping in one of the shanty boats, with orgies to right and left of us! At least that would be obvious uproar, not this creeping up of things that never came. I thought again of confetti, wistfully.

Later there was a thunderstorm.

Then I heard another motor's menacing sound, which I felt was rather more than I could bear. I tried to shame my panic by thinking of friends who had gone with their husbands to Africa or New Guinea. But, hang it, they'd been hedged in carefully by safaris. Our safari, what there was of it, was fifteen miles away.

Of course this was civilized country. Civilized? Ha! Read William Faulkner. Degenerates, murderers, idiots, in a swampy wood not nearly so big as this one. I'd take a good savage headhunter any time.

The motor died away and I lay still, dreading to hear it come back. It did. I gave a slight moan.

"What *is* the matter?" Lee muttered.

"Motorboats in my hair — Happy New Year, darling," I said bitterly. The chugging grew louder.

"Lee," I said desperately, "those boats are beating around like bats tonight. What are they after?"

"Nothing. Go to sleep."

"There isn't anything for them to look for but us. No houses or anything. Have you your money with you?"

"Yes, of course. But they're living their own lives. Don't worry."

Worry! Oh, no, I wouldn't worry. I would simply consider calmly the possibility of escape in the kayak. But we had no idea of the geography of this swamp; we'd never find our way out even if it ever grew light again. I grew tired of lying stiff, listening for pirates. I thought of pioneer women. There were bigger and better women in those days, I hadn't a doubt. Just the same I knew now how they lay listening for Indian whoops — like this. Reaching out my hand to them pityingly, I tumbled into sleep.

Crash!

It was outside, sharp against the tent. My heart jumped to my chin. Our Doom had come. It was the maniac, of course; a murderer wouldn't whang outside. In my sleeping bag I curled like a shrimp in despair.

"Owl — probably — after our ducks —" Lee murmured sleepily.

I have had happier New Year's Eves. I thought of Blake's

"Some are born to sweet delight,
Some are born to endless night,"

and decided the latter was certainly my fate. But the night did come to an end, even as the glacial period did. We were up and about at daylight on New Year's Day, a damp and foggy morning. I felt sprightly at my survival — the survival of the fittest, for you certainly had fits, Lee said — and when he wanted to go hunting without stopping for breakfast I agreed without a murmur, hastily took a bite of bread and cheese, and went along.

Down the misted river we paddled, in such darkness that we could hardly see the logs and snags in the black water. Somewhere a chickadee was cheeing in the clouded cypresses. We slid in to a bank on the timber side, and crept up by ghostly pin oaks. There was a long wait among the fog-white trees, while we looked as much like dead stumps as possible. Lee flattened himself along a fallen tree on the bank, crawled through the underbrush to a little pond, and finally got a double as the ducks flew up through the woods. Pride in the hunter, pity for the hunted — how instantly the age-old emotions swept me!

A squirrel began to scold frightfully, six feet above my head; the wind

30

ruffled my hair. I discovered that my feet and hands were half frozen and that I was hilarious on this foggy morning.

We went back by way of the willows to see the mallards sailing two by two again.

"The drakes are very gallant just now," Lee said.

"Gallant?"

"Don't you see that drake, how he turns and stretches his neck and fidgets? He wants to fly, but he won't go first."

"Why, the angel! Are ducks so courteous?"

"They're polite as the dickens in the courting season. And isn't his lady exasperating! She'd fly in a minute if she were alone. But now she knows perfectly well he wants to get out and she's acting indifferent."

"Isn't that true! She's waiting till the last second, and there he is with his hat in his hand, just like you when I'm saying goodby at a party."

As we drifted there, concealed by the buckbush, half a dozen wood ducks appeared, floating out from behind a huge log. How gorgeous they looked through the faint mist! Jeweled, in fact. When they preened themselves it was almost a surprise that the brilliant iridescence was feathered. It seemed to me they were much more self-conscious and artificial than our mallards, but I could hardly blame the beauties.

Back at camp we had an enormous breakfast to celebrate the New Year, after which our guide appeared to help us break camp. Then we took our way back through the flooded labyrinth again. Usually when we leave a place I find myself saying, "See you again sometime!" This time, passing each river curve, it was "Never again, thank God."

The houseboats appeared at last. There were people moving on the shore, voices calling, all the commonplace things again. I felt like a lucky fly breaking out of a spiderweb. There were mudholes and deep ruts, pigs and slippery corners on the way out, but oh the feeling of freedom when we got to hard roads and rice fields and wide-spaced sky again! Along the telephone wires sat gentle doves, pale rose and tan and gray. Flocks of car-

32

dinals flashed through the thickets, and blue-birds gleamed across the road. I could have shouted.

That afternoon the little Stuttgart hotel seemed as luxurious as Pierre's. I gazed from our window out over the quiet farming country and loved every inch of it. Never, never need I go into an Arkansas swamp again. Yet I wouldn't have missed it. I would do it all over again rather than lose the vivid memories gathered in such a desolate setting — the fragile azure and gold of a sunset sky flecked with wild birds, above that somber swamp; bright wood ducks flying down the dark lagoon; the pairs of mallards drifting through willow stems.

Now we were in Louisiana. We had driven that morning through a rolling upland country of pine woods, fragrant and windswept. Later the land flattened till it was absolutely level, with distant clumps of trees hull down on the horizon. We sped on through the sunny afternoon.

I had a wary eye out for Abbeville. That sordid room in Arkansas had sullied my perfect trust in places to stay all night. I had a horrid vision of bare dusty streets, unpainted store buildings, and a ramshackle hotel.

My forebodings were needless. We came into Abbeville in the late afternoon and found a charming blur of white houses, dense live oaks heavy with Spanish moss, holly trees, palms, and winding roads. The shadows lengthening across the quiet streets and the old brick courthouse drowsing in a peaceful square were just as they should be in a southern town. Everything seemed very still and quaint and little. And the hotel was modern.

Abbeville, one hundred and twenty miles west of New Orleans, is in the heart of that French-Acadian country through which Evangeline wandered, inexorably tracking down a Gabriel who surely was unconcerned about being found. West, north, and east of it is solid ground, except for a few cypress swamps. South of it the marsh begins.

This marsh stretches along the whole coast of Louisiana, a great belt from twenty to forty miles wide. Its southern rim ends in coastal islands,

34

thin lines of sandy soil which bar the sea from the swamp. There are no cities, no harbors, on this coast. The marsh itself is a vast extent of roseau cane and swamp grasses, broken by canals or natural bayous.

We were to go out thirty miles into the marsh to the Rainey Wild Life Sanctuary. We had the vaguest notion of what to expect. I could only hope I'd like it more than I had the White River swamp. In any case we had the tent and the collapsible boat, and felt prepared.

However, when Dick Gordon, the sanctuary superintendent, met us at the hotel he said that the sanctuary had an island built upon the marsh, with not only one house but two, as well as a watchtower and a boathouse. Furthermore we could take a cook along! I hope I didn't look too complacent at that news.

The next morning, lucent and springlike with a south wind, we found a small black Robert for a cook, and wandered down a lane, past a tattered mansion, to the river wharf where the *Widgeon* lay. Our belongings having gone on board leisurely enough, it was announced that something had to be done to the motor. Why are launch engines so much more mutinous than any other kind? We waited the whole of that golden morning on the grass of the river bank. But we spent it remembering lazily how bleak a January morning can be in New York, and felt contented rather than annoyed.

This was a pleasant little river, untidy with launches, mostly unpainted, and clumsy barges. A tiny Carolina wren sang in the willows, above drawling voices. Once an ancient steamboat with a rear paddle wheel came by, and a line of lighters. Cedar waxwings tilted their crests in the hackberry twigs over my head. It was a timeless spot; eons passed unregarded. I was sorry when it was noon and we had to go back to the hotel for lunch.

Early in the afternoon the motor capitulated. A French woman with assorted babies claimed a ride — the whole district seemed to depend on Mr. Gordon — and went down into the cabin. We took on packages for various trappers, our motor chugged and stopped and chugged again, and

we started off down the river. Willows, live oaks dripping gray moss, dark hollies, all came to meet us around the curves.

"Robert," said Mr. Gordon, "we might have coffee." What an inspiration! I decided I liked this pleasant, deliberate Dick Gordon.

Live oaks again, with wider wings of gray. Rough cabins somber under shadowy trees, tiny and dismal abodes they seemed to me. But then coffee came, stronger and blacker than even the coffee of New Orleans. After two cups of it I was sure that the cabins were often gay, with fiddles playing, after all.

We went down miles of river, the banks falling away lower and lower until at last they merged into roseau cane, a tall reed, yellow as corn in these winter months. Then our first Louisiana ducks flew over, black ducks, Lee and Dick Gordon agreed. Gray foamy clouds hid the sky now — there was only a hint of blue here and there — and we swung out into the strange and pliant marshes.

Under a darker and darker sky a long canal cut through the yellow reeds to the horizon. The wind turned cold, and we had another cup of coffee and then another, as we went on past the endless roseau canes.

Finally we came to the open water of Vermilion Bay. For some miles we watched a distant lighthouse across the gray expanse; the slow beat of the motor made me sleepier and sleepier. Then we had more coffee, and it was by far the most potent I had ever encountered. I felt wide-eyed now.

36

Back into the reeds again. The canal stretched interminably before us. What an uncanny land to find myself in! The gray twilight darkened. We stopped at a group of cabins built along the narrow levee of the canal, and as we let the Cajun (Acadian) family out we caught glimpses of heads at the lighted windows and dark figures at the water's edge. The French greetings came oddly to us through the dusk. Then we chugged on again through solitude.

By now the coffee had taken full effect. I felt like a loose engine bolt, clattering all through. I tried resolutely to keep my teeth still. Finally, "Home ahead." The marsh grass was pale in the night; the lane of water curved. Dark low buildings loomed on a shore, and a light shone out from the boathouse as we slid in by the dock.

We climbed out, I at least rather shakily, and were introduced to three black silhouettes, a French-Acadian couple and Dick's assistant, Nick Schexnayder. Nick, slight and quick and silent, took charge of the launch, and we followed our host. On the dim islet two roofs, several midget trees, and a skeleton watchtower were inked against the sky. A warm and rainy wind fluttered from the darkness.

Inside the house was bare, and clean with gray paint. We had dinner at nine and there was more coffee. But not for me. If I can't say when I've had enough, at least I know when I've had too much. However, dinner seemed to cure my vertigo, and I went to sleep with no trouble at all.

One should plan definitely to get to a strange place at night. When all the surroundings are unknown and waiting, the new morning greets one so buoyantly. I woke to a curtainless window framing a moment of peach and pale rose beneath a stern stretch of gray, and when I heard faint

quackings — and, I must admit, a call from Lee — I hurried out into the wind.

From our austere small island the marsh and water lay about us in far swaths of cream and taupe, pale green and lilac, under an immense and fragile canopy of light. Floating on the lake to the east, in the pure color of the morning, were wild ducks by the hundreds. Scaups near by, mallards farther out, and canvasbacks, conspicuous with their sharp red heads and white backs, still farther. This was what we had come so far to see, this serene haven. The cocky black and white scaups were even trusting enough to come sailing down the small canal by the dock. Red-winged blackbirds were everywhere, and the boat-tailed grackles performed absurd acrobatics in the reeds. There was a delicious cleanness in the flood of wind and sun over these level spaces.

The main canal west of the island ran north and south, like a solitary street misplaced, stretching to the horizon. An offshoot from it led to the dock and boathouse on our east bank. From that a short canal ran eastward into Belle Isle Lake through the orange reeds.

After breakfast Lee and I climbed the sixty-foot watchtower and looked out over this new domain. Gold grass and turquoise water — how utterly different from our black swamp in Arkansas! This was a two-dimensional landscape, with length and breadth but no height, guilelessly open to the sky.

"How big is the sanctuary itself?" I asked Lee.

"Twenty-six thousand acres; that's more than forty square miles," he said. "Paul Rainey had a game preserve here. After his death his sister gave it to the Audubon association for a wildlife sanctuary."

We looked about us. The gigantic circle of marsh was unbroken by a single tree; on every side of us it ran smoothly to the horizon, with only two or three dwarfed cabins of the trappers to give any variation to the carpet of reeds and water. I had a vague feeling that I had done this before — stood on a tower and looked out over vast level spaces. Where? When? Then I

remembered. It was Mont-Saint-Michel. We had climbed its marvelous tower of lace and looked out over the sands of Brittany.

What a contrast! Mont-Saint-Michel: an island of solid stone, a peak of granite, with the great abbey crowning it, the street of old houses circling its base. To be reminded of it by this island, a flat handful of clay and sand, man-made in this quaking marsh! I remembered how moved I had been when I looked down over the tidal sands of France to the same pale cream and blue which the eleventh century had gazed upon. Mont-Saint-Michel, drenched with worship and passion and danger in the springtime of our civilization, with its Norman arches, Gothic cloisters, and St. Michael triumphing above the lofty spire. And now I stood on this hasty framework, this pencil sketch of a tower, and was reminded of the Merveille!

40

Yet this view was stirring too, this width of grasses, with its absence of any history. An empty land, never peopled, whose only traffic, except for a stray pirogue, was in the vast galleons of clouds drifting in the blue air. This was a place owned by wind and wings; earth was strangely unimportant. Here was freedom. Not savage country, but unspoiled by man. One's spirit widened to the great circle of limpid air; one's thoughts flew out as swift and uncaught as the wildfowl passing.

Lee was occupied in trying to place the sanctuary. The northern boundary we could see. It is the intracoastal canal, which cuts across the whole state. The southern boundary, beyond our vision, ends at the gulf in seven miles of shell beach. Beyond the sanctuary to the east was the State Game Refuge of Louisiana, and west was a game preserve belonging to Mr. McIlhenny, who has made Avery Island such a successful refuge for egrets and herons. But of course these were artificial boundaries. The wide coastal marshes sweep uninterruptedly from the Mississippi to Texas.

And these marshes are the winter home of all the blue geese in the world. Dick said there were perhaps a million or so at the Mississippi delta, where the greatest concentration occurs. The sanctuary itself has from fifty to sixty thousand. The great flocks of lesser snow geese are farther west, in Texas and California; in Louisiana there are only a few to every hundred blue geese. There are greater snow geese too, but they winter along the Atlantic coast.

We waited there on the tower for a sight of the waveys, as they are called because of the long wavering lines in which they fly, so different from the sharp V's of the Canada geese. We were the center of an incredibly level circle over which bands of ducks flew far on every side of us. I scanned the flocks, looking for geese among them.

"Not there," Lee said. "Geese fly high."

I looked up. Above the range of the ducks was an emptiness of air, beyond which fluffs and billows of gray arched widely. Through rents in these cloudy reaches we caught sight of blue profundities, dazzling, endless. What a sky country! But we hoped in vain for a flight of geese across the cloud drift. They were already at their feeding grounds. We had to descend to earth with no glimpse of the ethereal trumpeters.

Lee brought out our collapsible boat so that we could start off to explore this strange land. Rainey has the launch, a speedboat (named the *Chick*, to rhyme with Dick and Nick), and rowboats. But we had carefully brought our kayak with us; it had to be assembled. We laid out all the pieces neatly on the dock, where sacks of rice (duck food) stood all about us, and began to put the boat together. This wasn't easy. The directions said it could be assembled in ten minutes, but it must have become swollen with pride in Arkansas. The French wife, Eve — and I wondered if that came from Evangeline — a dark, swift-footed girl who lived with her trapper husband in the smaller house below the tower, came over to laugh at our struggles. Nick too, who was investigating the launch (he was a natural mechanic, it seemed, and extremely clever with engines), kept an alert eye on us. We had the boat half finished when Robert came out, beaming, with eleven o'clock coffee. I had learned rapture, but also discretion. I took one small cup.

Our expedition finally started after lunch. As we paddled along the canal we met a muskrat trapper in his pirogue, coming in. This in truth was the arctic meeting the tropics, for our boat was modeled on the lines of the Eskimo kayak while the pirogue is a homemade dugout, quite like the *cayucos* we once saw in Panama. It is a very rude affair, just a log hollowed out, with the bow slightly pointed, and is extremely unbalanced, far more so than a canoe. In Carolina the negroes call them "trust-me-Gods." But from the trapper's expression he thought our craft the peculiar one. The two boats, in fact, were ridiculous together, one so much too long and narrow, the other too short and fat — Jack Sprat and his wife.

On into Belle Isle Lake we skirted the high roseaus. These reeds sometimes startled us by standing three or four times as high as a man. They have a long stalk, jointed like bamboo, with narrow leaves and a tasseled head.

In the winter months they are gold, old-gold, tan, or ivory, depending on the light. We edged the narrow canes, ducks glinting ahead of us. We began to flush unsuspecting birds as we paddled silently along. Lee made quick sketches of the way they rose when startled, the deep-water ducks aslant, the puddlers almost straight up. Belle Isle Lake, the largest in the sanctuary, was a mile long. From it we paddled through a bayou into East Lake, bouncing wildly through the windy water. Myriads of canvasbacks, mallards, and small teal sat half hidden in the waves or flew up from the

rushes. We discovered widgeon and gadwall too. At least Lee did, and I confirmed his opinion solemnly.

Inwardly I was appalled at the slight chance of my ever telling them apart. I felt dizzy in this merry-go-round of waterfowl; my head swam, far more erratically than the ducks did! Back to the ornithologies tonight, I thought sternly. Would I find myself regretting, after all, the White River bottom, with its untaxing duet of mallards and wood ducks? Mallards were easy to distinguish now. So were canvasbacks, of course, red-headed, with big white bodies. I could remember scaups, small and black-and-white, and pintails ended in a long spike. But after I'd been intelligent with all those variations, I felt that coping with gadwall and widgeon was excessive.

I tried to find a rhyme like the one Painted Jaguar used for the Tortoise and the Hedgehog, but what can you do with names like gadwall and widgeon! Except for pigeon, there's not a chance, unless you're an Ogden Nash. The best I could do was to make slogans for myself.

> *The widgeon wears a white wig.*
> *The gadwall's garbed in gray.*

And as for ever recognizing the females! To me the duck realm must remain strictly a man's world. I can never learn to distinguish one lady from another.

Lee made a few pencil sketches, here in East Lake. I sat in the bottom of the boat, holding it as steady as I could against the bank, listening to Lee's whistling and the rattle of the dry bulrushes in the fresh wind, and felt very amiable.

It surprised us to find how long it took us to return. It was quite impossible to judge distances because of the extremely low shores, with only reeds and myrtle bushes to give height. But there was no reason for hurrying. Imagine a world where there are no insistent appointments or errands! We didn't have an obligation; not even to hunt for wildfowl, for they were everywhere, making direct and exquisite patterns against the sky or on the water. To see them as casually as this was something I'd never dreamed of.

Out again before breakfast the next morning, above a high fog we heard the geese calling. It was the first time I had heard the cry of wild geese. I knew it was one of the most stirring sounds in the world, but I hadn't realized how it would besiege the spirit. It is to bird song what the trumpet call is to music, a gallant challenge and a desperate cry, lifting the heart, disturbing it.

Then the fog broke slightly and we caught glimpses of great wavering V's against the blue. Here was the vision we had sought — hundreds of blue and snow geese rushing south through the cloudy wraiths. It was worth our journey of two thousand miles to see these airy cohorts.

And, far as we had come, these geese had come farther. The fall flight of the blue goose is magnificent. It often makes a direct flight from the southern end of Hudson Bay, traveling day and night, rarely coming close enough to earth to be seen, until it reaches this coast.

The blue goose is one of the most glamorous of birds. It has been considered a very rare species; its elusive habits both in migration and in breeding have made it of especial interest. Even its wintering grounds were not known until a comparatively short time ago, and its breeding place was an utter mystery until 1929, when J. Dewey Soper first found it on Baffin Island. Now even the well-defined route of migration, down the east coast of Baffin Bay to James Bay and from there practically straight south to Louisiana, has been traced. It has a surprisingly small range after it completes its migration. Only two places on Hudson Bay,

Baffin Island and Southampton Island (where it was found by George Sutton), are its known nesting places; it winters only in this Louisiana marsh. The snow goose, too, breeds beyond the Arctic circle.

All through breakfast we kept rushing out to see more geese fly over. To Dick's amusement. To him we were as ridiculous as guests in New York would be if they'd rush out to see a bus go by. Sometimes the enchanting birds were close enough so that we could see them clearly. Sometimes they were high above the clouds and we could only hear the remote cadence.

That afternoon we went west, through a brown grass swamp, to see canvasbacks. Lee had noticed them flying west, from the dock. Down the main canal a mile or so we lifted the kayak over the high levee to a pirogue trail, a waterway like a footpath, so small that our boat just fitted in.

This tiny grass-grown canal gave an imitation of a brook sometimes and then changed back into a canal again, like an artless Dr. Jekyll and Mr. Hyde. Humps of muskrat houses dotted the brown landscape, and far off we could see the tiny figures of the trappers as they moved along their beats beyond the sanctuary boundaries. Down here you rarely see the muskrat himself, as you sometimes do in the north. He is far more secretive in this dense cover, a night worker.

In a clouded silver sky ducks flew past, high and black. Lee, pulling the

47

kayak along by brown grass stems in one place, almost put his finger in a small snake's mouth. After that he began to use his paddle again, and we emerged from our brook into a silent glitter of lake. Here we pushed our boat far into the canes and pulled the tan stems down over and around us. Only our heads appeared. I longed for a muskrat trapper; how amazed he'd look to see two bodiless heads staring at him. We sat there like small stone faces until our canvasbacks began to come in.

They came flying like arrows from the east, swift and sure. The canvasback is a splendid bird, with a slight menace no other duck suggests. Its ruddy head is pointed and severe, its white body with the black breastplate shipshape and compact with power. Even the whistle of its wings differs from that of the mallard's; it has a keen threatening note. Some ducks come down gamin-like, almost small boys sliding down a bannister; but when a canvasback comes in, wings set and fast, with feet sternly spread, it is as impressive as the landing of a Pilgrim Father. One bird came so near that it was a temptation to try to catch a foot. Then a Ward's heron flying up, stretching long neck and wings, assumed as he settled in the air such a compact smug expression that we laughed aloud. There was also the black dot and dash of a small snake swimming. Which made me remember water moccasins.

They are the most prevalent of the poisonous snakes in Louisiana. I looked about for a narrow something four feet long, dark and blotched with yellow, with a yellow band from eye to neck, looking the vicious and poisonous creature that it is. I also looked around for white patches marring

48

the landscape. Someone had told me this snake had the horrid habit of sitting coiled with its white mouth gaping, hence the name cottonmouth. And though it is supposed to be a water snake it has an unscrupulous way of climbing into bushes or reeds.

Here we were, wrapped in reeds to the chin.

"Perhaps we might try another place?" I suggested, after reflection.

Lee agreed. We might try walking in the marsh. Back we paddled to the stream and disembarked. Now I had on rubber boots so large that I walked around in the boots as well as striding with them. Therefore I went twice as far as Lee, in the same distance, pulling the reluctant boots from the sucking mud with hands and feet, and lagging far behind my lord. Soon I was left standing ignominiously in tall grass, with an uninspired view of a hen mallard asleep on a pond, and the sound of puddling and scrabbling somewhere to the right. I was also left with instructions not to move till Lee came back; the mystery of those sounds had to be solved.

There I stood, the little tin soldier red with rust. " 'Now don't you move till I come,' " he said. " 'And don't you make any noise.' " The wind moaned in the grass; a mist of rain enveloped me. After a time the situation ceased to be amusing.

I felt again the antagonism which solitary places have for man, that I had felt so vividly in Arkansas. Not the profound threat here which you feel from the sea, if you stop to feel it, even on the calmest day. Not the awful aloofness with which mountains can turn their backs on you. This was an insecure feeling. This quaking watery universe, this haven for hideous crawlers, where alligators slept under the gray water and snakes swam and twisted — this world repulsed me. I should have stayed where I belonged, on land.

No Lee came back. What now? Did I just stand on and on and on? Two marsh hawks, hunting, swooped madly over the windy plain. They weren't burdened with boots, I thought enviously. I felt like a tall turtle, below their fleetness.

Across the pond four pintails appeared. Pintails are the aristocrats of the duck tribe, and their slender immaculate grace, the elegance of their pointed tails and slim necks, made me forget my discomfort. Even when they stood on their heads, "up tails all," they did not lose their lovely distinction.

But it was dusk. Did I dare to call now? Duck shadows flew past into the twilight; I shifted in my vast boots; I was cold. A small panic seized me. Something must have happened to Lee. Alligator holes! they had told us to look out for those. Had he plunged in on an alligator?

He reappeared at last. With sketches and chuckling. It seemed that canvasbacks had been the cause of the commotion. Accustomed as they are to dive for their food, in this pond, though the water was only five or six inches deep, they were still conscientiously diving away. It was all very difficult. When the food bobbed to the surface it was usually snatched by a circle of irresponsible ringnecks, the laboring canvasbacks remaining slightly hungry as well as tired and cross.

I might have been a canvasback myself as we groped our way home in the dark, through mist that slanted into an icy drizzle. What a chilled and laborious way it was down the windswept canal, before we welcomed the oblong of yellow light awaiting us!

It was comfortable that night to have a wood fire in the stove and to get into slippers and light clothes. Dick told us entertaining stories of his boyhood in the great Kankakee swamps, before that wildfowl haunt was destroyed by drainage, and I read about canvasbacks in Phillips' *Natural History of the Ducks*. We stepped out, late, to see if the sky had cleared and were startled by fiendish screeches just over our heads.

"What on earth — "

"It's Tito," said Dick behind us. "He's a barn owl, and he thinks this place belongs to him after dark. Look, here he comes." In the faint moonlight I caught sight of a fierce little face between two feathery wings. It

looked like a devilish cherub. "We can't step out at night without being yelled at."

"Why Tito?" I asked.

"His scientific name — *Tito pratincola*. Tito is the only barn owl I've ever heard of to live in marsh grass down here. They usually choose cypress swamps or oak chenières."

"Does he really live in the reeds?"

"He did, but this winter I put a nest box up on the tower for him."

We heard afterwards that Tito was really Titania. Later in the spring she laid five eggs, and five small owlets hatched. Three of the young left the nest: one drowned in the canal, one, unluckily, in the cistern, and the third survived. What became of the other two? No dead chicks were found in the nest box. But when Dick cleaned the bones and pellets out of it he opened the pellets and there were the legs and feet of two young owls, neatly done up in those balls of feathers and bones which owls disgorge.

It seems that the barn owl starts incubating as soon as the first egg is laid, so the young hatch in rotation. By the time the last ones come out of their shells the first two or three are strong enough to seize most of the food. For this reason, usually not more than three survive. It was Dick's theory that the strong birds are also intemperate enough to snap up, literally, their little brothers.

On Sunday we went visiting after breakfast. All over the marshes along the levees are scattered the rude cabins of the trappers. Most of these men farm or work in small towns in the summer and come out to trap in the winter months. Some of them, however, live in the marsh all the year

round, in board shacks or on houseboats, and make a living in the summertime by fishing or shrimping. Usually of French-Acadian extraction,
though near the Mississippi they may be Spanish, a great many of them
can neither read nor write, and speak no English.

We went rushing along the narrow canals in the speedboat, with a great
wing of water whirling up from each side. Since Dick never condescended
to slacken speed it was exciting when we approached the remains of a
bridge, with just space enough between the heavy posts for our boat to
skim through. But we never scraped. Above the roar of the motor Dick
shouted information. Nick said nothing. He sat with his head cocked, like
an alert fox terrier, watching to see what interested us and what we missed.

At a decrepit wharf we stopped. Out came the bearded head of the
house and six small children of practically the same size. Out came the
wife with a tray of cups and the tin drip coffeepot which is used by all
Acadians. We had coffee in the boat, with the family in a row along the
piling watching us. We couldn't converse, except with Dick as interpreter,
but it was a pleasant visit there on the sunny landing.

The next cabin belonged to a solitary trapper who asked us to land for
an inspection of his two small rooms. One was a fur room with drying
racks on which muskrat skins hung. Each skin was stretched on a small

wire frame, a miniature sweater stretcher. Besides the muskrat skins the trapper showed us beautiful pelts of opossum, raccoon, and mink. To my surprise I heard that Louisiana leads all the other states in the production of mink skins. In the second room there was an unmade bed, a stove perched on wooden blocks, a table, and an old black rocking chair. Cans of food were stacked on a narrow shelf and a jug of whisky stood on a small box by the bed.

After we left Dick told us that Louisiana has three million acres of marshland which produce up to ten million muskrats yearly. There are twenty thousand trappers, almost all Acadians, and each is allowed by the law two hundred and fifty traps. The income from trapping is almost six million a year.

We traveled on with variegated stops until we came out into the pass, where porpoises swam and pelicans flew. On an old pier black snaky cormorants preened in the sun, and long skeins of geese were wavering back and forth over the bay. Here again the low banks were very deceptive. Some brown pelicans on the sand flat lurched up like steam shovels.

These brown pelicans were a special delight to me. I am not alone in this preference, evidently, for the pelican is on the Louisiana seal of state and also on its flag. In this state the brown pelican is a constant resident; the white comes as a winter visitor. This bird is huge, from four to five feet in length. The wingspread of the brown is seven and the white sometimes measures nine feet. In the great pouch which hangs from its lower bill it can store the fish it catches. Robert Cushman Murphy in his *Oceanic Birds of South America* gives a fascinating account of the brown pelican fishing:

"In the deep and clear cove . . . the brown pelicans would hurtle from a height as great as 20 meters above the water, usually spiralling or twisting on their downward course so that they struck with their backs rather than their breasts toward the surface. In other words, they would be gliding upside down, with the wings still half spread at the instant before the plunge. Usually they quite disappear, even to the tips of their long

wings . . . The twisting descent is doubtless responsible for the fact that the bird turns some sort of somersault under water and comes up heading in another direction from that of the diagonal dive . . . As soon as the pelicans reappear on the surface, they turn down the bill to drain the pouch which, according to Gosse may hold '17 pints' of water, after which they toss up and open the bill so as to release their victim, only to receive it in the throat and swallow it with a gulp. It is at such times that Laughing Gulls and noddies attempt to steal the prey of the pelican, sometimes standing on the latter's head."

Lee and I went out in the kayak after lunch into a Sunday-afternoon feeling that was strange in such a world. We were too lazy to paddle. We drifted in the shadow of roseaus twenty feet high.

Here the silver water reflected a deep bronze from the green-gold of the canes. Outside the cove lay a great semicircle of stainless blue, its delicate margins rimmed with gold weed. I felt as if I were in a sustained dream. A white ghost of a moon wandered among cloud wraiths in a turquoise sky and a little noiseless noise came from the immensely tall quill canes, where shadows were sharp violet. Now and again the breeze just touched our hair. What dim memories are stirred by wind touches, memories too small to recognize. An occasional quack was the only definite sound.

Small creakings, which were the ducks' conversational murmurs, came to us. It was so still that when a stray bird came down on the surface of the lake we could hear the little surge of water as it landed.

The scaups that usually stayed near the home canal came by, playing truant. I knew it was the same group because I had a favorite among them. He had lost an eye, but far from seeming pathetic because of that, he looked more rakish than any of the others. If there has ever been a swagger that duck had it. We named him Dick Deadeye, and expected him to burst out at any minute with "Sing hey, the merry maiden and the tar!" These scaups were a great contrast to the canvasbacks we had watched the day before. Instead of looking severe and purposeful, their slight crests gave them a comically inquisitive expression. I noticed that a ringneck who was with them had a higher crest, which sloped back to its peak and made this duck look even more impertinent than the scaups did.

Now and then we would see a small flock of ducks fly up from one pond to light down in another. They were especially joyful, these short flights. Not the steady flying of ducks when they are traveling, nor the panic escape from danger. These were play flights; somebody said "Let's go to the next pond for a bite," and they all whisked over. The unafraid darts and dashes were like random snatches of music through the afternoon.

At sunset a gray cloud bank threatened the clarity of primrose in the west. As it grew later the sky thrilled with more color, apricot with small curlings of flame; and the ominous cloud became a fog bank of chrysoprase, shot through with light. The wind was strong behind us and to my delight I found that by using our paddles for sails we could let it blow us home. A half-moon sailed overhead, very high. There was a lovely, faintly luminous look to the whole landscape as the sky faded to strange hints of rose and lemon and chartreuse, haunting the water. We felt triumphant blowing down the lake, our paddles held stiffly vertical. Even the sight of Eve, doubling up with laughter at our sailboat, did not diminish our pride.

When we landed at the house the red-winged blackbirds flew up in

56

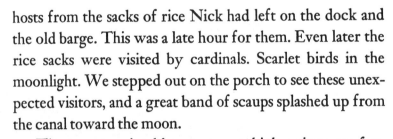

hosts from the sacks of rice Nick had left on the dock and the old barge. This was a late hour for them. Even later the rice sacks were visited by cardinals. Scarlet birds in the moonlight. We stepped out on the porch to see these unexpected visitors, and a great band of scaups splashed up from the canal toward the moon.

The next morning blue geese very high, going very fast, flew over Rainey in hundreds, their cries coming down to us only faintly. I took my cup of before-breakfast coffee (Dick's bad example) and went out by the tiny chinaberry trees. A flight of snow geese came past, much nearer than the blues. They were glorious things in the misty sapphire air, silver with black wing tips, tracing diaphanous patterns through the faint fog. The blue geese were dusk-gray with white heads, and as decorative as the others though not of such fragility.

Later, as we traveled south down the main canal to Pearson Ponds, the geese, lost now in gray clouds, were still crying overhead, a lofty accompaniment to our paddling. They were later than we usually heard them. Lee thought they might have lost their way in fog. They fly from their feeding grounds to gravel beds and back again; their diet of tough roots makes them need plenty of sand and gravel for digestion.

Holes of fiddler crabs made polka dots in the black banks as we went along, and deserted bird nests starred the myrtle bushes. Then we discovered a tree! — a willow tree, a very thwarted one, only a few feet high, but still an actual tree, the only one in the miles that led out to the sea. It looked as stark and lonely as one egg in a refrigerator, but we regarded it with profound affection.

Farther along we dragged our boat over the high dike into the first pond. This was a different type of marsh; short bunches of salt grass, couch grass, and hog cane, which looked much like a coarse rice plant, varied it. Here we saw for the first time the three-square grass which is the food of the blue geese. Its stem, evenly triangular, grows from two to three feet high. It is usually found in solid stands, acres of it, but here it was mixed in with the other grasses. Here too were coffee weeds, huge, ungainly, and unmarshlike plants with long brown pods, which are crowding out the grass in many sections. Muskrat houses abounded in this region.

We followed small channels from one pond to another. One pool was edged only with salt grass, hairlike and short. After the harshness of the other marsh plants, the coarse textures and rank stalks springing from the mud, this pale green brevity was an incongruous bit of elegant garden here. In another pond the growth of cattails was extremely heavy. The heads were broken down over the water in a dense canopy. We pushed our kayak far in under the tangle and sat in ambush, completely covered to the eyes.

There was a long space when nothing happened. The fog had gone; it was a hazy day of gray and blue, and hot, now that we were sheltered from the wind. Small triangles of the broken reeds stood in the pond about our hiding place, drawn very correctly, as if someone had been doing geometry problems there.

If we had only known then how the Indians make blue goose decoys we could have made some there. Not long ago we saw in New York the magnificent all-color film which Martin Bovey has made of geese in Hudson Bay; it shows the Indians setting up lumps of mud, in one end of which they stick two long white feathers. These look surprisingly like blue geese at a little distance. White bags stuffed with grass imitate snow geese feeding. I wish we could have tried such decoys at Rainey.

But I did not mind the emptiness; I felt quite contented. For this was somehow a marshland in time as well as in space. One is usually conscious of a current to a week, a contour or a motion in time; we had no such feeling here. There was a tide in our daily life of course, but such an imperceptible one that it had no pressure or urgency.

At last visitors came. A widgeon paddled up, full of self-importance, going to a directors' meeting at the very least; settling his feathers, swinging his tail, he bustled along. Black ducks surprised us, and green-winged teal shot past; two shovelers came flying, close enough for me to see their spoonlike bills. Then an egret alighted, like a spread flower, on the cattails near by. I hardly had time to gasp at its beauty when I caught sight of two more white and long-necked birds across the pond.

"Two more there," I whispered.

"But those aren't egrets," Lee said. "They're immature little blue herons. Their feet are green."

"That sounds illogical," I objected.

"If you see a white heron with green feet it's a little blue. Just remember that. A real egret has a yellow beak and black legs. But the snowy egret has a black bill and though it has black legs its toes are yellow."

"Stop it!" I said urgently.

"It's not really hard. Little blue — white when young, greenish feet. Got that?"

"Yes, but I resent it. Why can't it make up its mind? If it's a blue heron, why not *be* blue?"

"Remember it's only a little blue! The egret has straight white plumes and black feet."

"I can always think of this beauty," I gazed at the bird near us.

"Snowy egret. Snow-white plumes — they're curved back at the tips in the nuptial plumage — yellow feet. They sometimes say it has golden slippers, which fits in with its air of elegance. And you can remember the whole bird is lighter, in more ways than one. It is only half as large, and it is a purer white."

"White can't be whiter than white."

"Oh can't it? Remember Whistler's portraits? The snowy egret is the whitest bird on earth. Don't forget, too, black feet go with yellow bill, in these birds; yellow feet with black bill."

"They do it on purpose," I lamented loudly. To my embarrassment the egret curved its graceful neck to look our way. I felt apologetic and greatly at a disadvantage, clothed in cattails as I was. But it was a delight to be a part of the marsh like this, even if we were the submerged tenth. Our egret stood on tiptoe, and was gone.

Drama entered now. We saw a duck hawk strike and cling to a scaup which kept struggling on in its flight in spite of the attack. The hawk suddenly lost its hold and the released scaup fell swooning into the tall bulrushes. I was afraid it had been wounded, but Lee thought it was not seriously injured. We saw no more of it; the hawk continued on his way refusing to look crestfallen.

I had hardly caught my breath when a blue goose came, low over the cattails, straight at us. Larger and larger, till we could see the red rust on its white head and neck, its dusk-blue feathers and pinkish legs folded back, its slightly open mouth, even its serious expression. It might have been making the apology I once overheard from a man in a telephone booth: "Sorry, I'm going to be preoccupied tomorrow."

The goose flared at the last minute, when it saw us. I felt snubbed; we belonged here too. In Arkansas I had felt we were truly aliens in a strange

place. But here was fellowship — we were friends, house guests, in fact, on the birds' own land. "Perhaps we had better go," I said haughtily. To the goose; but Lee thought I meant it, and we crashed suddenly out into the world again.

On the way back "There!" Lee said. Several white dots appeared ahead of us. He pointed to one on the left. "That's a snowy egret, I'm sure. The rest are herons." How could he tell? But he was right. Soon we could see it plainly. I had always thought that the flowers of the white phlox were the most dazzling white in the world but this snowy egret matched them.

When we pulled our boat back again over the levee I stopped on top of the dike to look around this tract of our dominions, to savor the wide restfulness, the release that comes to one in unpeopled places. I gathered it again, treasured it, the secret ecstasy which a solitude may yield. I remembered snatches of Lanier's *Hymns of the Marshes* —

> " . . . *this silence, filling now*
> *The globèd clarity of receiving space,*
> *This solves us all* . . .

and

> " *'Tis here, 'tis here thou canst unhand thy heart,*
> *And breathe it free, and breathe it free,*
> *By rangy marsh, in lone sea-liberty*."

Only — strange, I thought, the secret is not the one we found in our canoe country and in our English forest. Why? I know serenity here; not peace, exactly. But I liked it! I looked down at our small cocoon of a boat, waiting to take us along the taut ribbon of water; I looked at the gigantic expanse of naked sky about us. Oh yes, I liked it here!

The afternoon turned gray and raw with a north wind. We went with Dick and Nick to the traps to see them band the ducks. This is one of the minor activities of the sanctuary. About six thousand ducks have been bedecked with small aluminum bracelets at Rainey. When a band is put on a bird's leg its number is sent to the Biological Survey in Washington; and, the bird coming to an untimely or a timely end, if the number on the band is sent in, the place and time of death can be compared with the place and time of banding, and knowledge of bird wandering acquired.

The trap we visited was across Belle Isle Lake near the north shore. It was made of chicken wire with a small funnel opening, so arranged that once the carefree ducks entered, following a trail of rice, they were unable to find the opening again. This woven wire trap, covered over the top and staked so firmly to the lake bottom that nothing could escape, was in about two feet of water. It was quite large enough for Nick to enter easily. He began to fish the ducks out with a net and hand them to Dick, who shoved them into burlap bags.

64

The gray afternoon became vivid. There were about a hundred ducks in the trap, and the shimmer of canvasbacks, the green heads of the mallards, bright wings beating, spray flying, made a brilliant kaleidoscope.

"Do you ever catch anything besides ducks?" Lee asked Nick. Nick was beginning to talk to us a little by this time but he let Dick answer most of the questions, and Dick replied to this one.

"Lots of fish. Raccoon sometimes. The raccoon swims around the trap trying to get at the ducks inside and when it comes to the funnel it goes right in."

"Is it too frightened to bother the ducks, then?"

"No, it will kill from four to seven. But when it can't get out afterwards, it certainly gets wild. Remember the first time you found one, Nick?"

Nick grunted.

"Nick went in to bring the coon out — we're supposed to let them go — and he tangled up with that coon! I didn't know for a while who was going to bring who out of the trap. But we've learned. Holding one under the water for a while with a board does it a lot of good. I'll remember this in case I ever get married."

When we had five bags full of ducks we took them back to the sanctuary and the men began to band them on the dock. One by one they were pulled up out of the sacks — it was like the grab bags we used to have at parties when we were little — you never knew what was coming next, a redhead, a pintail, or a scaup. Dick snorted as one hen mallard came out. "She gets in at least once a week," he said scornfully. "Regular martyr type."

Dick held the birds, Nick snapped on the bands skillfully, and Lee recorded the numbers in a notebook. The bands were small aluminum rings stamped with numbers and the words "Notify Biological Survey, Washington, D. C." They were split along one side so they could be spread apart, slipped about the shank of the duck's leg, and squeezed shut again.

After the ducks were banded they were tossed into the air, and flew off looking rather dazed from their strange adventure. Sometimes they were so draggled and bewildered that they toppled into the canal after a flap or two, but as a rule they flew straight into freedom.

And still we had not seen the wild geese close at hand. So on another morning we went to the sea edge, out to Chenière au Tigre. The day was almost violently beautiful. The strong burnt-orange of the grasses, the metallic blue water, clashed like cymbals about us. We sat on the roof of the launch dangling our feet, letting the wind whip our hair and sting tears to our eyes. The roseau leaves were like tournament banners flying.

Seven miles of marsh and then we came to Chenière au Tigre, the oak-ridge of the tiger. How thrilling it was to make a landfall, to see a long island of firm ground rise from the blowing rushes! And here were trees again. I hadn't realized how I had been missing branches against the sky until we approached the land and I saw the leafy arms of the live oaks spreading their wide shadows about them. Chenière au Tigre is a long and narrow sand ridge along the ocean's rim, separating the sea from the marsh. This strip may have a bit of history (besides its natural history, which is all that the rest of the marsh can boast). Pirates and smugglers, even Lafitte's company, may have landed here, since they ranged all along the Gulf of Mexico.

I fell in love with the island immediately, being susceptible to islands in any case. Among the live oaks was nestled a little settlement, quaint and primitive. There were even horses here, and cattle. However, there were also wild hogs. Dick Gordon failed to tell me about those until we had left the boat and taken a muddy road through palmettos and cacti. Then he spoke carelessly of boars so dangerous that they attacked men on horseback, and told briefly of a meeting he had had with one himself. He had had a gun. We had no weapon.

The road changed to grass, and behind canopies of live oaks we could see a gray-violet sea, smooth as satin. I forgot to walk in wary scallops or scan the landscape for a galloping pig.

We passed a queer little cemetery under green trees weeping with the Spanish moss. It had a picket fence and the graves were covered with neat oblongs of shells. Each had a cross at the head with a broken glass tumbler hanging upside down from its arm.

Most of the straggling houses were enclosed by fences too. The hotel, set back among fig and orange trees, was a low white building, really only a long cabin with a veranda. Its door stood open; there was a rude fireplace with a driftwood fire, and very simple furniture. The hostess offered us coffee as soon as we appeared, and then we strolled in the citrus orchard till noonday dinner, which we had in the kitchen with two young school-teachers and the children of the house.

After dinner Lee and I set off, determined to have a close sight of wild geese. The high shore, a sandy ridge along the gulf, was bordered by live oaks which were almost excessive in their use of moss festoons, by palmettos, cacti, and mesquite, which seems to have migrated here from Texas. Prickly pears were here, and trees of ironwood, locust, red haw, and hackberry. On these beaches the small perching birds come to rest after their long flights from South America on the spring migration. The shore birds for which this area is famous were not there in the great numbers we had hoped to see.

We walked east, counting the white pelicans that were flying over the gulf. It was low tide and very placid. Mud flats extended far into the gulf. A bar, so far out that the breakers could barely be seen, separated the inner lagoon from the gulf proper much as coral reefs do.

The white pelican is extremely graceful in the air. He does not dive into the water for fish as the brown one does; I have read somewhere that the reason he can't dive is that he has peculiar built-in water wings, air sacs under his skin, which keep him afloat. But if he does not dive, he can mount

69

to great heights, and often soars in circles for hours at a time, too high to be seen except through binoculars.

When we walked on again, I began to find tracks of hogs, after which I observed with scientific thoroughness all trees even faintly climbable. Soon we began to see our waveys, flying up along the horizon. Then, looking over the ridge into grass marsh, we could see the geese feeding far off, beyond the cattle.

The birds were eating the three-square grass, which grows in the brackish water back of the gulf. We had been told they like best of all the sections that have recently been burned over, and will fly miles to find such places. In the autumn, if there are no burned areas, the huge flocks will settle over the tall grass and flatten it with their wings. The birds in a solid mass hover over the grass and gradually settle as they beat it to the earth. Sometimes the geese feed in one spot until all growth is killed and every root is pulled up and eaten. Then what the Cajuns call a *crevey* is formed, sometimes several miles long, and this bare area often changes into a shallow pond. In any case it takes years before the grass grows there again.

70

As we walked along the ridge the voices of thousands of birds ahead came to us in a roar. Lee began to plough through the sand faster and faster. Just then an enormous sow stirred lazily behind a log. A litter of pigs surrounded her. Then in among the bushes a great yellow boar moved. No razorbacks here; he was the shape and almost the size of a hippopotamus.

"We'll make a detour," Lee said blithely.

"We'll make a return," I replied. "You know they're most dangerous when they have a family. I'm not going to be in that cemetery with a glass tumbler over me and an embarrassing inscription about pigs."

But Lee convinced me, with some difficulty, that a detour was safe if it was wide enough. The wideness of it led us in among the cattle. I preferred them to pigs, and Lee was delighted. He said being mixed up with cows gave us a far better chance of getting close to the waveys.

Nearer and nearer we came to the great flocks. They had told us there might be from thirty to sixty thousand here, packed into a square mile. Soon we could see the individual birds, splendid in the sun, all facing into the wind, stepping forward with dignity. They fascinated us, these massed birds, walking there on the sea plain. They kept close together and they all seemed to shout at once; these geese are very conversational and not at all repressed. The clamor was worse than a mile-square cocktail party.

And not one of them seemed to like to be the last in the flock. Every few minutes a little group would fly up from the rear and alight in front of the huge crowd. They drifted down very gently with a lovely slow-motion effect, surprisingly graceful in contrast to their clumsy walk. Through the glasses we could see even the vertical crinkles in the white satin of their necks, their pink bills, the brightness of their eyes.

I don't know why birds and beasts are so touching when they do not know they are observed; human beings aren't, except very small children and those one especially loves. But any animal leading its little independent life stirs a feeling of pitying reverence.

As we watched there larger flocks of geese began to take wing. "It must be time for them to go to roost," Lee said. They rose in irregular flocks, shimmering in the low sun, and then straightened out into long triangles and bars and curves. How beautifully, how *wildly* they took flight!

It was high time for us to fly too. Reluctantly we turned back, to meet Dick at the launch.

We stopped a minute on our way home at a trapper's cabin, where muskrat skins hung on stretchers along the levee and an old houseboat lay abandoned in the scum of a bayou. The trapper took us into his shack to show us with pride some exceptionally fine mink skins. He asked Dick if he would take the load into Abbeville on the launch and my eyes opened wide when they decided gravely that these valuable skins must be put in a tow-boat behind the launch, since the launch itself was so gasoline-soaked that it might easily catch fire. My valuable skin hadn't been put in a towboat.

On our way home the evening sky was supremely, foolishly beautiful, decked out in petaled clouds. As we sat cross-legged on the roof of the launch watching the bright rose and apple-yellow a north wind ruffled the pink water ahead of us. Terns flew around us. These birds are airier than the gulls, at once sharper and daintier. Their flight is full of wit, it is rep-artee with actual wings; gull flapping is sedate beside it. Terns flirt across the wind, slender of wing and bill and body, their black caps and forked tails giving them a distinction that makes the gulls seem robust and blunted. We saw egrets again, small ghosts in the darkening marsh. A line of snow geese flew over us in a widespread curve, blush pink in the last light from the sun. And when we reached home, with appetites fanned by the night wind, Robert had deviled crabs and chicken pie for supper. It was a most successful day.

I spent that evening over duck books, though I hardly needed to look up our distinguished feathered friends by this time. After I learned to recognize ducks swimming, Dick and Lee gave me a strenuous course in ducks on the wing. How could anyone tell whether a minute speck far in the air was a gadwall or a black duck? And even when they were closer they insisted

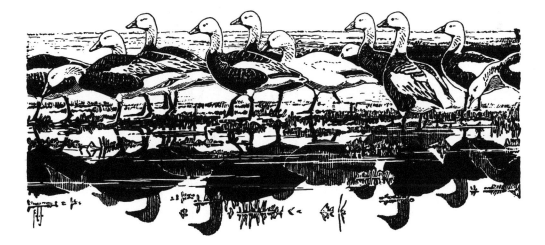

on looking like entirely different ducks, in the air, from the kind they were on the water. But I learned.

While I was reading, Dick asked me about a baldpate. I looked blank.

"Same as a widgeon," Lee explained.

"Oh, that's not fair," I cried indignantly. "As if one name a duck wasn't enough!"

"It makes your slogan easier to remember," Lee consoled me. "If a widgeon wears a white wig it's because he has a bald pate."

"I don't like the precedent," I said firmly. "I also wish to complain to the management about gulls. When I'm trying desperately to decide what duck looks so strangely white, and then it turns out to be a gull, it's most disconcerting. We don't need gulls here anyway; I can see them in New York."

The days went by serenely. There was only one flaw. No matter how a conversation started, sooner or later it changed into ducks. However adept Circe was at changing men into beasts, I'm sure she wasn't half so successful as these men were at turning every topic into ducks. I made a rigid rule that ducks could not be mentioned before breakfast. All day, all evening, if necessary; *not* before breakfast.

I liked waking at Rainey. Our bare window filled with an unflawed morning, rosy-pale or copper-bright, the little song of a marsh wren and quacking far away, the sound of oarlocks as Nick started off with bags of rice to bait the banding traps.

I liked strolling on our tiny domain before breakfast, such a small walk around our island, the virginal world about us; seeing the canvasbacks and mallards stream down the marsh; watching the grackles sit on the reeds pointing their bills straight up into the sky and gargling exuberantly, or fluttering their wings and clattering in their idiotic way; being aware of vibrations from the stalks and narrow leaves surrounding us, of the multitudes of little lives — plants, insects, amphibians, birds, so many levels of existence — hidden in the few feet of height this island attained; aware above all of the great dome of air about us, crystalline, carved with bright wings.

Since some visitor had thoughtfully built a blind of roseau cane at the end of the minute canal which led to the lake, I decided one morning, while Lee went tramping in the muskrat swamp, that I would photograph ducks from it. There were usually about six thousand ducks around Belle Isle Lake; I ought to get pictures of a few. I wrote these notes that morning in the blind.

"Behind the roseau blind. Past yellow stalks the gray water is dotted with black and gray scaups. They stayed away in a wide semicircle as long as I sat on the box. Now I'm crouched rabbit-like on the ground, and they're slowly drifting back, the chunky rascals, their heads high, a wild look in their eyes. Here come some, very close! I can see their little topaz eyes, their comic alert expressions. They jiggle in the gray waves with their reflections lengthened by the ripples.

"Just now ducks were all around me. I could see every feather blow up in the wind, every shimmer of green and purple on the black heads! Beyond the others floats a solitary canvasback, his head a geranium-scarlet in the momentary sun.

"I don't know how I feel about this place, really. Just here it's snug, with reeds to shut me in, and the scaups small and likable. But when I'm alone on the marsh itself, it seems too flat a solitude!

"And all our ways are waterways. It is interesting to go everywhere, even the shortest distances, by boat, but I miss tramping. There's only the levee to walk along, and what is the use of walking when there is no destination to reach? I wish we had some snowshoes to try; a Dr. White used them successfully on this marsh. Nick is a wonderful marsh walker, like a cat, but we've been warned that he takes a quiet delight in luring visitors on long walks cross-country, where they flounder deep in the mud while he skims maddeningly ahead.

"I think this country divides my emotions. I am half attracted and half repelled. Its horizontal beauty grows on me. But the knowledge that there is no solid surface to the earth, in all these miles, gives me an insecure feeling. And there are no dark tones anywhere. Everything is very pale in color. When the reeds do have shadows they are violet or tan or green, not black. Can you cleave to a country which has no deep shadows?

"I noticed yesterday the coarse textures of the vegetation, but I didn't think then of its brittleness. There is nothing I cannot break with my two hands. I think of the forest wilderness, of the subtle gradations of pasture land, of mountains muscled with iron and silver. But this country with no rock-ribbed foundation — I can see how it can fascinate you endlessly, how you can come back to it again and again; an unreasonable magic pervades this unflawed air. But a strong affection and loyalty? I don't think so. I must ask Dick — "

Here Lee appeared. He had been part way along a trap line with a trapper who walked fourteen miles a day on his beat. They had waded marsh ankle deep, knee deep. Sometimes they had tramped the levee and sometimes they were in saw grass above their heads. That morning they had captured fifteen rats, a coon, and a mink.

In the afternoon Lee and Dick went to Hell Hole in the speedboat, with black storm clouds boiling up all around. But having decided it was excessive to worry when they'd deliberately chosen to go to Hell Hole I had afternoon coffee with Eve, and then turned to catching crabs again. Robert had shown me how the day before. Tying a fish head to a string he lowered it into the canal, and when a crab caught hold he lifted the string and scooped his victim off neatly with a net. It was hardly game fishing but it amused me.

So I went to him again for bait. He had no fish head, so he generously parted with the little foreleg of a muskrat. I didn't like that foreleg from the first. But I went out on the piling and sat down on its edge. The sky was very black now with a lurid yellow in the far southwest. Clouds rushed by, just over the roseau flags, and the wind slapped the water viciously against the posts. I threw in my bait and waited, then pulled it up through the brown water. It came to the top forlornly, a ghastly little arm and hand. Almost human it looked, that small hand.

I suppressed a shiver and plunged it once more into the water. Then I found I couldn't bear to pull it up into sight again. It looked too much as if some dwarf baby had lost it. That was nonsense, fantastic nonsense. Concentrate on the crabs, I told myself sternly. The jeweled blue and orange of their claws was marvelous to see. But when the crabs came up they'd be hanging to that pitiful small bone, and the tiny hand would curl, half open —

I gave up crab catching.

I went over to the old barge and sat on it, watching the red-winged blackbirds swirl in the stormy wind. The clouds were scudding fast across a low sky. The marsh shivered.

I curled up in a shelter made by piles of rice sacks, and as I opened *Remembrance of Things Past*, which I had brought along, I thought how unreasonable a choice it was, having no possible connection with this country. But it was an interesting contrast, to read the intricate and fastidiously wrought prose in such an uncultivated setting. Then I came to Proust's description of the Guermantes Way, along the Vivonne River. I stopped and read again the passage about the water lilies and their pool.

"I have seen in its depths a clear crude blue that was almost violet, suggesting a floor of Japanese cloisonné. Here and there on the surface floated . . . a ring of white petals. Beyond these the flowers were more frequent and . . . disposed by accident, in festoons so graceful that I would fancy I saw floating upon the stream, as though after the stripping of the decorations used in some Watteau festival, moss roses in loosened garlands. Elsewhere a corner seemed to be reserved for the common kind of lily, of a neat pink or white, like rocket flowers, washed clean like porcelain, with housewifely care; while a little further again were others, pressed close together in a floating garden bed, as though pansies had flown out of a garden like butterflies and were hovering with blue and burnished wings over the transparent shadowiness of this watery border; this sky-ey border also, for it set beneath the flowers a soil of a color more precious, more moving than our own; and both in the afternoon, when it sparkled beneath the lilies in the kaleidoscope of a happiness silent, restless, and alert, and toward evening, when it was filled like a distant haven with the roseate dream of the setting sun, incessantly changing and ever remaining in harmony, about the more permanent color of the flowers themselves, with the evanescence and mystery — with a quiet suggestion of infinity; afternoon or evening, it seemed to have set them flowering in the heart of the sky."

I looked out over the dull marsh. It too would glow like that, in summertime. Only instead of one small pool, or two, there would be countless miles of petals. Immense, unbelievable gardens, garlanded with white lilies, lilac with water hyacinths, rosy with mallows —

Just then, in the wharf's piling, I saw tiny petals. I had been dreaming of leagues of blossoms, but here was an actuality. It was, to be sure, a rather scrawny little actuality, like a first unlucky attempt at a goldenrod, but it was April's own yellow, on the fifteenth of January!

Enraptured, I shrieked for Eve. "My first spring flower! Look! Oh, it makes me frantic; think of the millions there are to see in summer."

"Also millions of alligators," she reminded me. "Also millions of snakes. Great clouds of mosquitoes blow toward you across the marsh. For hours you will breathe those mosquitoes."

She elaborated till I began to think we had been right, after all, to choose January rather than June for these spacious water pastures. She told me that the lilies, as they call the water hyacinths, are an annoying weed along the whole coast. They came from one man's garden in Florida: he grubbed them out of his garden and threw them impatiently away, and that was like letting a genie out of a bottle.

The hyacinths grow so fast that they choke the canals, not only in the marsh but far up the rivers inland. The floating masses jam the waterways until boats cannot make their way through. Then the government sends steamboats out to spray poison over the plants, which sink into the river bottom. Dick obtained the poison formula from the government, and now, using a tree sprayer mounted on the launch, he murders hyacinths wholesale.

Cattails too and other reeds fill the ponds in summer. The men used to pull these plants out by the roots until they discovered an easier way. Now they go into the marsh as soon as the water has become warm in the spring and cut the cattails about a foot below the surface. The plant, unable to get air, then dies of suffocation. In about three weeks, when the men go over the area a second time and cut the few survivors down, the pond is neatly cleared. This has to be done every three years, however, as the grasses grow in again from every side.

The storm clouds went sweeping off to the east. Eve and I climbed the watchtower to see if the speedboat was coming back. We could see a solid block of rain slanting down on Vermilion Bay, and all the east was sooty black, but the western sky shone clear and pale under the rim of the last dark clouds.

Eve amused herself by pointing out to me the locations of alligator holes about the sanctuary. But I was far from satisfied; a sudden desire to see the alligators themselves seized me. Though they are in half-hibernation through the winter they sometimes crawl out into the sun when it is warm. I insisted on being shown an alligator.

"Wait with patience until the summer," Eve mocked me. "And also then you see alligator eggs, thirty or one hundred in a nest."

"What kind of a nest?"

"Of grass and mud built above high water. The sun hatches the eggs — that is not so boring for the mother. Better than a bird's plan, I think? Sometimes Dick has brought eggs to the house and made a nest himself for them in the sun. From time to time he throws a pail of water over them. Then in a few weeks — baby alligators!"

"Very little ones?"

"Oh about eight inches when they come out of their eggs. And very clever! They take care of themselves from the first. But the mother alligator stays near. They are not an indifferent family. Sometimes if they live on a pond where there is space the last year's children, two or three feet long, are still with the mother when her new babies hatch."

As we watched there on the tower, new storm clouds reared against the clear west. Far down the canal we could see a small black speck which was the speedboat coming home. We clambered down to welcome Dante and Virgil back from Hell Hole.

I asked Dick about alligators at dinner that evening. "Haven't you seen one yet?" he said, evidently feeling responsible for the omission. "How would you like to go out tonight and pull one up from its hole?"

"What do you mean?"

"We can go out in the launch with the light and a pole, just as we do when we hunt. But we won't shoot — alligators are usually killed in summer and anyway we don't shoot them on the sanctuary. Of course you can pull one out any time, but they look fine at night, dripping up out of the black water with the light on them!"

It sounded fun, I said.

"You don't want to pull a sleepy alligator out of bed for no reason at all," Lee expostulated.

"I do! I want to see how it feels to pull on an alligator!" I said ruthlessly. "Even if you are on the animals' side, you might be inconsistent about an alligator!"

Nick didn't say anything, but he brought out the gator poles, slim ones about sixteen feet long. Each had a strong iron hook at one end. With that the hunter hooks the alligator in the mouth, when it snaps at the pole. As the head is pulled above the water the alligator is usually shot, but here the natives kill their victim with an ax or a long-handled hatchet. "One man can pull out a seven or eight footer," Dick said.

"I'll be perfectly content with a two-foot specimen," I said modestly. "In fact, I couldn't think of accepting a larger one."

We were ready to start forth when rain descended. Not a gentle shower but windy torrents. "It'll rain like this all night too." Nick was disgusted. So instead of chugging out after big game we sat around the stove and talked about it, while the rain beat like surf against the walls.

"Alligators are still plentiful," Dick told us, "though they've been hunted for years. I've often wondered how an alligator can dig a hole in this hard clay — sometimes his den is twenty feet long. With his front feet so far back and his legs so short, I couldn't see how he managed to dig at all. Finally I began to notice that the big ones had hard clay on their noses sometimes. So I've decided they must bite the clay out."

"And they go in their holes tail first," Nick added dreamily, "so they can come out teeth first."

"Sometimes you find the hole in a shallow place," Dick went on. "Then you have to stand in water as deep as three feet to pull the gator out. I don't know anybody that's ever been bitten, but you can get knocked down when the gator starts on his way to freedom."

"Oh yes," I said, "Do you remember that article 'Getting the Gators' — Alfred Bailey wrote it —"

"Then it must have been about this country; he's written a lot about Chenière au Tigre," Lee said.

"He told about his guide getting stuck in the mud when he was trying to pull a nine-foot alligator out of just such a hole. The alligator decided to go away from there and in getting out it stuck between the guide's legs. Then neither one dared to move an inch for fear he'd arouse the other! They stayed there frozen with fright until Mr. Bailey got tired of waiting and offered to stir the alligator up a little. The guide didn't approve of that idea, and finally he grew so frantic that he shot himself straight up in the air out of the mud."

Lee looked pained. He always feels responsible for the accuracy of the scientific facts in my stories. (They're *our* stories, he feels, and he prunes them thoughtfully when they show undue exuberance. Of course I feel responsible for his, too. He dislikes exaggeration and so when he tells about being in a hurricane you gather, with some difficulty, that there must have been quite a breeze; I like to whip up his stories. In both cases our efforts are apt to cause sparks which seem to arise from friction, though really they fly up from fires of deep loyalty and helpfulness.)

"He couldn't shoot himself straight up out of thick mud," Lee said.

"Yes, he did."

"He wouldn't even be able to crouch down before he jumped. He'd crouch on the alligator."

"He shot straight up from fright," I insisted. "The way your hair stands on end when you're frightened, only more so."

"Without even pulling on his bootstraps, I suppose," Lee said resignedly. "You read that article again."

"Mr. Bailey said it was ridiculous," I offered.

Dick laughed. "Anything can happen with gators. I once had a seven footer come alive after I'd shot him and was hauling him into the boat tail first. He came to all at once. He turned on me with a snap of his jaws and drove a wicked set of teeth deep into the side of the boat. So I let go of what I had of him and shot him all over again."

"Tell them about the tarpon," Nick said.

"That was queer," Dick admitted. "Well, when I came here we had to kill off some of the alligators, there were too many to cope with. So during one summer we killed about three hundred."

"With hatchets?" I asked.

"No, we were shining their eyes at night and shooting them with a small rifle or shot gun. Animals' eyes don't shine in the dark, no matter what people tell you, but they do reflect any light. An alligator's eyes look like two balls of fire floating on the water when they are within range of our searchlight.

"We used a small gasoline launch with one man to drive and one to do the shooting. One night two of my boys started out to shoot gators shortly after dark. In about half an hour I heard the boat coming back, but there was no light from it, so I went out with a flashlight to see what the trouble was. What a looking boat! The boys were blood and slime from head to foot, scales as large as a silver dollar all over the place, a split gunwale, one man with a broken rib. And a big fish story, though no fish. In going along a flat just at the edge of deep water, the noise of the motor had scared a big tarpon. It started for deep water and the boat was in the way.

"Imagine going along in a boat on a dark night, two men perched on a narrow bench, and a hundred and fifty pound tarpon suddenly sails inboard, strikes one man in the ribs, knocks them both down, mauling hell out of them, sends the light overboard.

"They were in pitch darkness then. The tarpon jumped over the engine into the after part of the boat, after that, and the boys staggered up. Just then that fish hopped back over the engine and knocked them down again. Another good drubbing, and then Mr. Tarpon went on his way. All quiet on the western front, no light, no fish, nothing but a lot of blood, scales, and slime. One busted rib."

Perhaps it was just as well it had rained that night, I thought.

I was ambitious the next morning. I was sure I had taken some good pictures of scaups the day before; I wanted even better ones that day. Better than anyone had ever taken! I wanted portrait studies; I wanted to catch the impudent gleam in their eyes.

But after waiting hours in the blind I had only two snapshots, not good at that. The ducks were all idiotically cautious that morning. Heads high, giraffe-necked, they circled nervously just on the edge of my range. They kept up their tense hyperthyroid look all morning long. I longed to shake them till they looked as unself-conscious and contented as the mallard couples in the Arkansas willows. In fact I began to wish I could shoot them with a gun instead of with a camera. Infuriated as I was I remained patient. Far too patient for my own good. For all the rest of the week, whenever I'd see a scaup a dart of irritation would snap through me.

After lunch Lee saw some shovelers alight in Belle Isle Lake. Since he had been wanting to sketch some we crossed the canal in our kayak and

landed in the roseaus. They grew so thick just here that it was difficult to push our way through them; we were held from the water only by their broken mats. The reeds crackled under our boots, speared up like lances into the sun above us. The hotness of the afternoon made me wonder, but with only a feather of a qualm by now, if moccasins were stirring.

Occasionally we stuck in the mud; we crashed along with far more commotion than we wished and at last found ourselves at the lake's rim. But beyond the saffron grass the metallic peacock water was empty and deserted. Above the roseaus thunderheads of cream ballooned about the sky, shadowed in hyacinth and powder blue. Terns flew recklessly about, their pointed wings sheer against the piling clouds.

Then from beyond the tall stems to the north ducks began to float out, as gay a pageant as one could ask. Mallards and ringnecks first, a few pintails, then a canvasback. Pintails again, their white vests flawless in the sun. Then Lee's shovelers came, one after another, in a single line. In spite of their peculiar bills they were beautiful birds, with their green heads and bodies of green and white and cinnamon. They swam briskly along, their heads low, skimming the water with their wide bills. A mischievous ringneck seemed to take great delight in getting in their way.

We stood in our boots watching these wild creatures feeding unconcernedly, tipping up, diving, flapping vigorously. Sometimes, tucking their heads under their feathers for a short nap, they rocked like anchored launches on the miniature waves.

It is no wonder that ducks and geese have always appealed to man's imagination. For one thing, they are so much their own masters that simply to get near them gives one a feeling of intense triumph. But their particular fascination is the power compact within them. Charged with energy as they are, their smallest motion is electric with zest; their swimming and their flight, even the turn of a head or a wing stretch, show an excess of vitality. There is a contagious exhilaration in such quicksilver life.

The ducks slowly floated out of sight around a curve of reeds. Lee was finishing his sketch and we were about to go when a solitary little figure came drifting out from the tall grasses. I laughed the minute I saw it. Such a funny squat little duck, and it was fast asleep! It floated slowly along, turning in a drowsy circle, its eyes tight shut. Once it almost bumped into a post and then, its eyes still closed, it paddled madly for a minute and went drifting on again.

"What is the silly?" I begged.

"A ruddy duck," Lee said. "But he has several nicknames. Sleepyhead — that fits him now. Then there's butterball, and dipper and dapper and dopper, and dumb bird —"

"Oh, no!"

"— and bumblebee coot."

"That's the name for him! I thought myself if he had to make a noise I was sure he'd buzz instead of quack!"

"Tough-head, too, they call him. He's hard to kill. And he has a habit you'd like. If he doesn't want to dive he sinks down out of sight, tail first, like a mermaid."

"The duck!"

"When he's courting he spreads that fool tail like a miniature turkey's fan, and puffs out his breast the way a pouter pigeon does. Then somehow he swells out above his eyes till he looks like a frog."

"Are you making this up? Imitating a turkey, a pigeon, and a frog all at the same time must be a little strenuous." I could not bear for the vision to disappear. "My bumblebee coot," I murmured, looking after him as he twirled sleepily along. This was one of those sudden infatuations so difficult for anyone else to understand. Sadly I crashed my way back to the kayak. I knew I'd never be lucky enough to see him again, and I never did.

Lee and I paddled on down the intracoastal canal. As we passed the Rainey sanctuary sign we saw a kingfisher perching on one end of it and a sparrow hawk on the other. What an advertisement it would be if they could be induced to sit there habitually!

We came back again at sunset. A golden sunset, a golden world. The tall roseaus shone gold with wine-dark shadows, the sky was faint green-gold above them, and the silent water, deeply golden too, had bronze reflections. Far ahead of us a pair of widgeons, glinting in the sunset, floated across our path, their wake a long ripple of golden fire.

I was conquered. I had resisted this land of half-submerged loveliness far longer than any other. I had held off from its strangeness. But after tonight this too would be my country.

As we paddled silently on the glory lessened, second by second, changing to soft honey-color, ivory, and dim brown. Something moved in the reeds we were passing, and between the slender canes a deer looked out at us.

A deer! We didn't believe it.

The delicate ears lifted, the soft eyes gazed at us a moment, then the apparition faded back into the reeds.

"Nick!" I cried as soon as we landed at Rainey. "Nick, we saw a deer!"

"Sure. There are plenty around," he said calmly.

"I don't see how deer can live here," I said.

"There must be almost a hundred on the sanctuary," said Dick, coming out of the boathouse. "Sometimes at night one will come out right back of here, get our scent, whistle, and charge off again. Several years ago," he went on, sitting down on the porch steps, "we had several days of hard blow from the east and finally on the last day the water reached real flood stage."

"It sounds queer to talk of floods here."

"No. The whole country was two to three feet under water, and the deer came west ahead of the flood. They piled up along the canal where the top of the big levee was just clear."

"Many of them?" Lee asked.

"We counted forty-four deer within three miles of camp, some with right small fawns. One old doe had twins and the boys got ashore and caught one. They petted it a few minutes and it followed them clear back to the boat. They'll become pets at once, those fawns. Seemed a shame not to take that little fellow, but of course we had to leave it with its mother."

After dark that night I went out on the island to see the full moon rising. The marsh was grape-blue, the gigantic moon threw a glitter of evanescent coins along the water. I decided to climb the tower and see more of the moonlit marsh. Just as I reached the top and looked out over the misted grasses a pelican flapped slowly across the moon, silhouetted against its golden plaque. The only pelican I ever saw at headquarters; I was deeply grateful for its moonstruck appearance.

I sat down on the top step of the tower, turning my back on the moon, and looked up at the stars that stood about me. Here was the most profound peace. How many unknown millions of people, I wondered, leaning my head back against the rail, had found this peace in a starlit night, above a fluctuating world of events, as I above this fluctuating marsh! When was it man first looked up at stars and found his heart at rest? How primitive was he, how different in his emotions from us, that first time?

I swam off into space and time so far that it was a relief to look down and see dim roofs and a bar of orange light cast from some hidden window — our roofs, light that belonged to us. A murmur of well-known voices: they were probably discussing ducks. No, I wouldn't go down quite yet.

Through the blue moonlight the west wind poured by me in a strong tide. The tower and I made the only obstacle to its rush, the only little eddy in the countless leagues of translucent flow. It was a delight to break that dark purity as it is a delight to walk in crisp untrodden snow.

At last the time had come for us to leave the sanctuary. We were to go into Abbeville for a dinner party, and the next day we planned to visit a gun club west of Rainey. We folded up our collapsible boat with great regret. No more hiding under the cattails in it, or flushing ducks from the reedy shores at twilight. No more voyaging in it down the tiny pirogue trails or along the wide canal. No more snow geese shouting above it through the heights of heaven.

It was storming again — Nick said we were in for a three-day north-wester this time. Dick was doubtful about Vermilion Bay, for sometimes so much water is blown out of it by a north wind that the launch cannot get through.

We left Rainey that morning in a gray drizzle. Both Dick and Nick were taking us in, and a queer uncouth trapper appeared out of the mist in his pirogue and joined the party at the last minute.

It was so foggy that we could not see the feathered squadrons on Belle Isle Lake nor any lovely lines of blue geese cutting the sky. But a few scaups in the small canal made a farewell committee — to my delight Dick Deadeye was among them — and Eve waved goodby from the rice sacks.

The wind-bent roseaus were almost gray in the raw morning. Water lay low in the canals; the small bayous were almost empty. At last we reached the shallow opening into Vermilion Bay, and scraped as we went over. Then came a wide expanse of cold waves. Hardly deep enough to float us, Dick said. We went slower and slower. Near the light, at the north end now. Very near. Soon, if we were lucky, we should be safe in the deeper water.

Then we stuck. We could hear our keel grate on the shell bottom. We backed off and struck once more, harder this time. I looked at the dim shore line through the rain.

"What will we do if we can't get through?"

"If we stick we'll be here till the water comes back. Maybe tomorrow," Nick said.

We tried another channel. It grew colder. My teeth chattered with the chill. The trapper, cross-eyed and stubbly, came up from the cabin

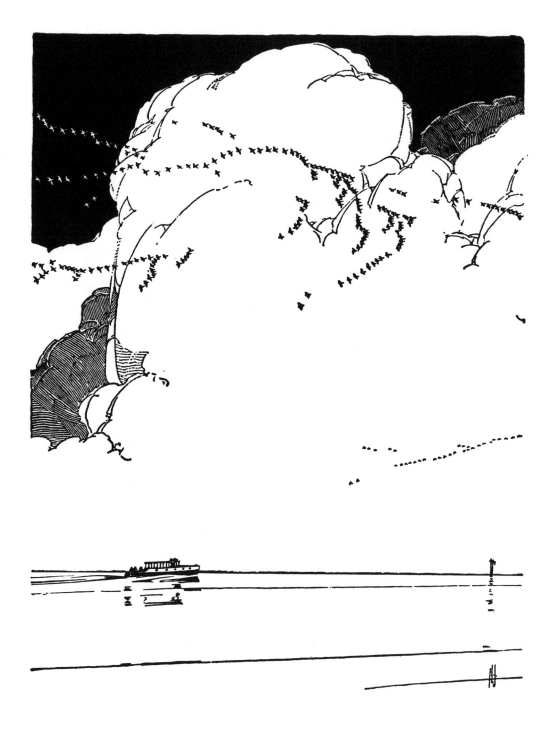

to look around, and his wild French didn't reassure me. Dick and Nick consulted.

"I'll try backing," Nick said. "If I can find mud bottom the propeller may dig us through." He turned the boat and we tried once more, backing like a crab. Stuck again! We couldn't stay in this chill bay all night. Not with a special dinner waiting for us!

Another try. Slowly, slowly we crept on. "Only forty feet to make," Dick called encouragingly. Near the light buoy we stuck once more. How unattainable that shore looked!

Another start. A scrape. A jar.

"Now we're safe. Twenty feet of water here."

What a relief! Nick was my favorite mariner. We had a cold wind-swept ride up Vermilion River, with blue herons standing in icy meditation along the bank, their wings in their pockets. At last we were under the bridges and at the city wharf.

How miraculous it seemed then, to come to a big white house, warm and candle-lighted, set firmly among massive live oaks, on solid land! Our host and hostess were from New Orleans, and we had the New Orleans bouillabaisse they had promised us. This famed fish concoction we had had both in Nice and New Orleans, but this evening it surpassed itself. It might have been the sherry added instead of white wine, or the pinch of saffron put in at the last, our hostess said. Or it might have been the narrow escape we had had from damp starvation.

After dinner we had coffee which I shall never forget. This was the *café brulot* — I had heard in New Orleans of its magic. A huge silver tray was carried into the drawing room, not by an old negro butler, I must admit, but the silver *brulot* bowl and great silver ladle were authentic family heirlooms. There were also hot coffee, brandy, sugar, and a dish containing lemon and orange peel, cloves, and a few coffee beans and aloes. Our hostess put all this into the bowl except the coffee. When the candles were blown out, she dipped up a ladleful of brandy, put a lump of sugar in it, and lighted it. The ladle lowered into the bowl blazed up with a blue flame. As she slowly poured the coffee into the fiery bowl and then dipped up the flaming liquid it streamed from the great ladle in a cascade of blue fire. When the light died the candles were lighted again and the coffee was served. I would journey to Louisiana any time for another cup, though its strength kept me so wide awake all night long that I began to feel I had no eyelids to close!

We went west from Abbeville, to a shooting club near Florence. This is a commercial club where anyone can go, but the season had just closed and there were no other guests, though the guides had not yet departed. I'm sure they did not count on women guests, but they made me very comfortable.

The rain poured down steadily as we set out in a launch from the end of a casual road, where we left our car standing in the mud and mist — by this time it was used to being abandoned. For several hours we rode in a battered launch without a top, mere packages of tarpaulin.

Along these gleaming canals the predominating duck was the pintail. I was glad to have a chance to see more of this slim beauty. It is fastidiously trim, a dandy of the old school. The narrow white stripe in its slender neck gives it the appearance of wearing a stock; one almost expects a quizzing glass. We might look draggled and disheveled in the rain, but not these pintails. Their delicate white and gray was in its usual perfection.

At last we came to eight or nine tiny cabins high on stilts above the water. This was a much more aqueous place than Rainey; there was no firm ground at all. Wooden walks above the water connected the various cabins and the cookhouse. At first I thought it was a rather dismal little place, entirely surrounded by rain. Not only water on all sides of us but above and below as well, as though we were amphibians.

But when we found our cabin at the end of the stilted line it was a good little cabin, staunch and well built. Really rainproof, too, I was glad to see. In the fireplace, paneled with pine boards, a wood fire flared; I began to feel gay again. The bunks along one side of the room, two above and two below, looked quite nautical. We had a washstand, a cupboard in the wall, ladderback chairs, — and a radio! And from the open door we could see arrowheads of geese, Canada and white-fronted here, crossing and recrossing in the mist.

This marsh was an entirely different type from that at Rainey, fresh water instead of slightly brackish, which accounted for the difference in geese. The whole area was flooded just now to a uniform depth of eighteen inches, and the soil was a humus into which a pole could be pushed. The rankest growth was cut grass, which alternated with a shorter light-colored grass so that the result was a blended pattern of the greenish brown ridges and the pale tan of the short grass, with open water at intervals. The only relief to this monotony was small groves of cypress, far in the distance, straight and without Spanish moss — tiny pencil scratches against the horizon.

In spite of the rain we set out to get a glimpse of geese. Mr. White, the oldest guide, took me in his pirogue. I had longed at Rainey for a ride in one; here was the fulfillment, and I felt triumphant as my overalled gondolier pushed me out into the canal. Another guide made ready to take Lee out.

"I'll take it alone," Lee said.

"Strangers cain't handle 'em," the guide protested. "Too tricky, 'less you know 'em."

"I think I can manage," Lee answered, and prepared to take over.

The guide disappeared into the cookhouse, we heard a shout, and immediately the whole troop of guides oozed unostentatiously out of the cabin and leaned casually along its wall. Having no idea that Lee's second home was a canoe while he was growing up, they wore expressions of pleasant anticipation. But to my pride the pirogue did not throw Lee; there was no sudden splash nor even acrobatics. He poled skillfully out behind our craft, and the guides vanished noiselessly with their blighted hopes.

Pirogue trails leading from the club to the hunting grounds had been cut through the grass, and we followed one. There were no cattails here, no roseaus or bulrushes; only a small lily pad sometimes varied the mat of grasses. Lines of geese strung the horizon, small groups were lighting down to right and left. The distant calls, carrying far through the damp air, seemed deeper and even more mysteriously poignant than the blue geese cries. I could understand now why they are invariably called clarion cries. No other word describes them.

"Will the geese be feeding together, the way they did on Chenière au Tigre?" I asked.

"Not now, missy," Mr. White answered. "These bad rains have flooded everything. The geese must be sick of water."

Geese are grass feeders, and of course spend much of their time on land, much more than the ducks do.

"Then how will we see them?"

"We're going to a blind," Lee said. We turned from the straight trail and went along what Mr. White said was an alligator path. Soon we came to a goose blind, hidden and carefully shielded by tall grass. Our two pirogues just fitted in.

There Mr. White proceeded to call down the wild geese. At his perfect imitation of the Canada's "Au — unk, — au — unk," we heard, out of the gray rain, a wild answer which always made our hearts leap. Then a great goose circled closer and closer and finally came across just over us, giving us a glorious view of the black head and neck, the white chin strap, and the gray body with darker wings. They seemed to me the most enor-

mous birds I had ever seen, fabulous creatures, as they loomed above our flimsy shelter.

Of course I had seen Canada geese on the Atlantic coast, but never near at hand. Even Lee had never been at such close quarters with the magnificent birds. We were breathless each time they passed, their powerful slow-beating wings blocking off the foggy light above us.

White-fronted geese came by too, though not so near. They were about half as large as the Canadas, practically the size of the blue geese. Their heads and necks were gray with a brownish tinge, the breast irregularly blotched with black. I had supposed they were called white-fronted geese because their breasts were white, but the name comes from a band of white feathers which encircles the pink bill. Their call is more of a harsh clang, a wah — wah — wah, instead of the long honk of the Canada goose. In fact the bird is sometimes called the laughing goose, though to me it does not have the hilarity in its note that a loon has.

Canadas came down in open water ahead of us, and I was amazed again at the buoyant way they had of alighting. It seemed to me the great geese came down so much more easily than any of the ducks did, a strange thing for these heavier birds. I was to notice the same thing later with the wild swans of Mattamuskeet and Currituck, along the eastern coast. It was a most enchanting sight to see those great white flocks alight on the faintly turquoise water. They came down as lightly as blown petals, the shadows on their slim bodies and silvery pinions changing from lavender to blue and back to lavender again. It seemed unbelievable that such imperial birds could sink down more gently than our small scaups had.

When we came out from the blind at last, I changed over into Lee's pirogue, and Mr. White went off to inspect some mink traps. I say "changed over" casually, but that is arrant modesty. For remember the pirogue is only a shallow length of log, precariously balanced, and I was deep in boots, corduroys and heavy raincoat! Added to that, two males were watching me sceptically, thinking "she'll never do it." It is one of the high

moments in my life that I alighted successfully in the second pirogue — if not as gracefully as the geese came down, at least with more certainty than I had expected.

Lee and I pushed into long grass and watched the geese as they flew by in long processions. The water had the gray greenness of mimosa leaves, with silvered wires darting through it where stray ducks swam. It had no sound here, any more than the Rainey canals had. I never seemed to get used to the absence of sound in the Louisiana marsh water. I had always associated the sight of liquid surfaces with liquid sound. Such silent water seemed odd to me, to the very last.

"Geese are the wisest birds I know," Lee said, breaking the stillness.

"More than black ducks?" I asked, remembering his admiration in Illinois.

"The black duck is wary, but these birds are intelligent," Lee said.

"What about crows; they always say crows are intelligent."

"You can't compare the two," Lee answered after consideration.

"Could you say crows are clever, but geese are really wise?"

"That probably expresses it as well as anything."

"What about owls?"

"Did you ever hear of a saying, comparisons are odious? But I'll tell you about geese and ducks. Say you're stalking them and they catch sight of you. If you keep coming, ducks will fly. But if you disappear from sight, they forget about you. Geese are different. When they see you, you can keep on coming; as long as you are too far away to be dangerous, they'll sit tight. But if you hide, they'll fly. Your disappearance constitutes a peril, for they don't know where you've gone or what you're doing. Geese are great birds."

Labyrinths of horizontal vastness lay quiet around us; the huge-

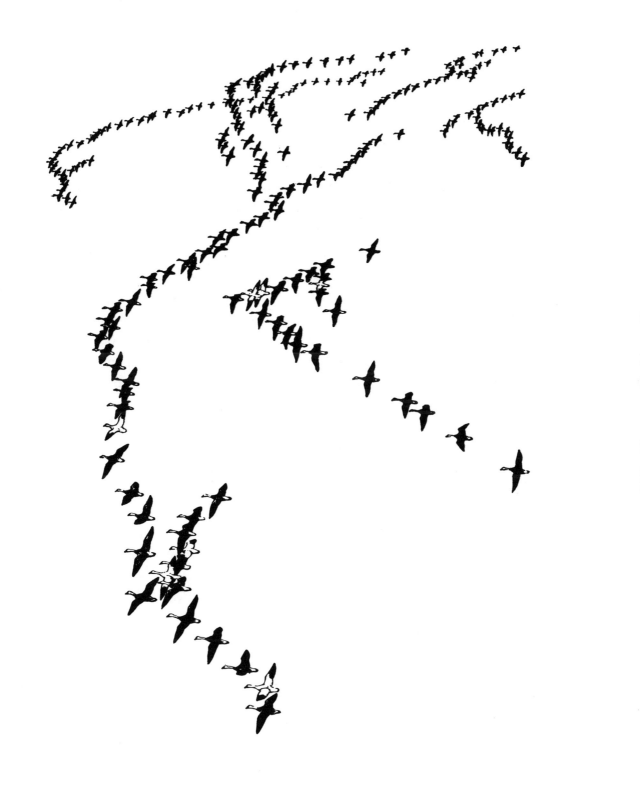

wrought clouds swinging above began to lighten and lift; there was a clarification of light. The canal turned to a silver pathway. A kingfisher darted brightly down the water, inspiration itself, and two brown sparrows followed after, like sober little second-thoughts.

At last clear gold claimed the whole west. Turning to the east we encountered radiant luster. A great rainbow stood against the dark storm, with a wedge of geese flying high through its arc. "Can't do better than that!" said Lee, and turned toward the shacks.

Supper in the cookhouse that night was rather an ordeal, for the guides wouldn't eat with us, or eat at all till we had finished. Our French and English didn't mix, but I would have been more comfortable as a halting conversationalist than as a spectacle. However, we could see through the window a changing sky of crocus and nasturtium, thin washes of scarlet and luminous green which darkened to storm again, and so we forgot the embarrassing silences. Still, we hurried through supper, and retreated considerately to our cabin.

Here Mr. White and another guide, both of whom had hunted on these marshes for thirty years, followed us, after their supper, and in the firelight they told us tales of the old days when ducks and geese swarmed here by the millions and the great cranes danced fantastically on the marsh grass.

That night I was very comfortable in one of the bunks, in spite of the feather bed. The firelight flickered on and on, the rain tapped loudly on the roof with its tiny heels, and at long intervals my heart quickened at the faint wild call of geese through the night. I thought sleepily but gladly of the hundreds of miles of fog outside with wild birds winging through it — friends of ours.

FLORENCE PAGE JAQUES (1890–1972) was born in New York. A poet and nature writer, she collaborated with her husband on eight books, including *Canoe Country, Birds across the Sky, Snowshoe Country, Canadian Spring, As Far as the Yukon,* and *There Once Was a Puffin and Other Nonsense Verses.*

FRANCIS LEE JAQUES (1887–1969) was born in Aitkin, Minnesota. His art is world-renowned, with major collections housed in the Museum of Natural History in New York and the James Ford Bell Museum of Natural History in Minneapolis.